ETIQUETTE TODAY

In the same series

Wedding Etiquette Properly Explained
Best Man's Duties
Sample Social Speeches
Wedding Speeches

Uniform with this book

Where to find *Right Way*

Elliot *Right Way* take pride in our editorial quality, accuracy and value-for-money. Booksellers everywhere can rapidly obtain any *Right Way* book for you. If you have been particularly pleased with any one title, do please mention this to your bookseller as personal recommendation helps us enormously.

Please send to the address on the back of the title page opposite, a stamped, self-addressed envelope if you would like a copy of our *free catalogue*. Alternatively, you may wish to browse through our extensive range of informative titles arranged by subject on the Internet at **www.right-way.co.uk**

We welcome views and suggestions from readers as well as from prospective authors; do please write to us or e-mail: **info@right-way.co.uk**

ETIQUETTE TODAY

Moira Redmond

RIGHT WAY

Typeset in 10pt Times New Roman by Letterpart Ltd, Reigate, Surrey.
Printed and bound in Great Britain by Cox & Wyman Ltd., Reading, Berkshire.

The *Right Way* series is published by Elliot Right Way Books, Brighton Road, Lower Kingswood, Tadworth, Surrey, KT20 6TD, U.K. For information about our company and the other books we publish, visit our website at www.right-way.co.uk

CONTENTS

Part Four: Communications and Class

INTRODUCTION

There are two common views of etiquette today. One is that it's all very old-fashioned and nothing to do with the way we live our modern lives. The other is that etiquette is a way of tripping people up and catching them out: that correct manners are a mysterious secret code which normal people have little chance of getting right – and when they fall into some cleverly-prepared trap they will have given others the right to despise them.

I strongly resist both these views. Of course, ideas of correct behaviour have changed since our grandparents' times, but today's logical and flexible rules are appropriate and helpful for our own age. And these manners are never used as an excuse to sneer or laugh at you or at others. The etiquette outlined in this book is designed to make life *easy*, not *difficult*.

In a social situation you have never encountered before (perhaps you have a new friend from a different background whose home you are nervous about visiting), then manners are not the means by which you will be caught out. They are the means by which you can be confident you are behaving well, allowing you to concentrate on getting to know your friend's family.

If you learn a few simple rules and try to act with kindness and consideration, you will have a set of manners that will take you anywhere in the world, in any company.

Note: Most of today's rules are the same for men and women. Occasionally I will address the sexes separately, but generally in this book I have used he, she, host, hostess, randomly and impartially to avoid constantly saying he/she, him/her, host/hostess. Unless otherwise specified, advice applies to both sexes.

PART ONE
SOCIAL LIFE

1

BASIC GOOD MANNERS

You may think you can run your own day-to-day social life perfectly well without any interference from me: you may feel that etiquette only applies at a higher level – very formal events, the party at your boss's house, Ascot. In fact, on those occasions the rules are probably simpler and clearer, and it's much easier to ask about them.

Small-scale social events can be more difficult because you're not sure of the rules, you're anxious not to do the wrong thing – or you fear that you have done the wrong thing – and you worry that you'll be laughed at even for asking. But there are a few ground rules which will take you through most situations, or at least give you some idea of how to cope.

Don't Underestimate Your Own Importance in Other People's Lives

By that I don't mean that you should imagine that everyone's in love with you, or longing to see you every minute of the day. But people hate one particular kind of rudeness: 'They didn't let me know they weren't coming/They didn't let me know they were coming,' can stand for all these complaints.

I'm sure there are some selfish, thoughtless people who couldn't be bothered, or forgot, but plenty of others just don't think that their presence or absence might matter to other people.

Listen to this: JANE: 'Mike said he'd drop round this evening. So we were in anyway, but we decided not to have coffee until he came, and we didn't start watching the film on TV, thinking we'd not see it all, and he didn't come, and didn't come, and then we weren't sure if we should go to bed because he might still arrive. It was really irritating.'

MIKE: 'I know I'd said I'd drop round, but it never crossed my mind that they might alter their plans. I just assumed they'd get on with their lives as if I wasn't coming, and that it would be making too big a deal of it if I actually rang to say I was caught up somewhere else.'

That's a small example, using a very minor social event, but you may get the point: Mike didn't have enough confidence in his importance to Jane. And even for a dinner party, plenty of people think it won't matter if they cancel so long as they let the hostess know. Of course, sometimes there are really good unavoidable reasons for cancelling, but, sometimes, well . . . People think it's just one fewer person to cook for, but before dropping out you should think (have faith in yourself) that it might be putting your hostess out considerably. She might be relying on you to be a good conversationalist or joke-teller or even a good listener. She might have someone special lined up to meet you . . . (Hostesses who want their revenge on cancelling guests who are single and fancy-free need only say, to women, 'Oh, what a pity, that'll leave me with far too many men – I was counting on you to cope with at least three,' and vice versa to men.)

So for all social events you should:

Say promptly whether you're going or not, don't break that except for a very good reason, and keep the host/organizer informed of anything relevant at all times and as soon as possible.

And this does apply to everything. Of course, it's more important for a formal seated luncheon than for a night out at the pub, but it still applies. Phone if you're late or can't come to something, even if it was an informal arrangement. You might be surprised: people even worry, think you've been run over, if you don't turn up. In these days of answering machines, you can, cravenly, ring when you hope they'll have left for whatever it is and leave your apologies on the machine. I can't quite approve of this, but it's better than nothing – it's not knowing that drives people mad.

Old-fashioned Manners: the Non-sexist Versions
There used to be many traditional rules governing how men behave to women, and they can seem very old-fashioned now.

It isn't wrong for men to continue with these punctilious politenesses, and even the most feminist of women should never be rude or ungracious to someone who is merely trying to be polite – it isn't an insult to have a door opened for you. And, on the other hand, a woman should not see it as an immediate sign of rudeness and a bad upbringing if a modern young man is otherwise polite and thoughtful, but doesn't treat her as a piece of porcelain who can't manage anything for herself.

Old Rule: Men always open doors for women.

New Rule: Whoever is leading the way, or is stronger or more capable of opening the door, does so. So you, whether man or woman, hold the door for those who are elderly or disabled, or are carrying small children or shopping – it doesn't matter what sex they are either. Otherwise, whoever goes first passes through, but then holds the door a moment longer to help the next through. Anyone who has been helped in this way says, 'Thank you'.

Old Rule: Men rush round a car (which naturally they have

Fig. 1. Always hold the door open for anyone less able than yourself.

been driving) to open the door like a chauffeur for a female passenger.

New Rule: The driver – male or female – opens the door from the outside for a passenger to climb in. At the end of the journey, the driver would open the door for and generally help an older or infirm passenger, but otherwise could safely assume most people can cope on their own.

Old Rule: Men give up their seats on public transport to women.

New Rule: Younger, fit people of either sex give up their seats to those less able to cope because of age, ill health, pregnancy or heavy burdens.

Old Rule: Men stand up when a lady enters or leaves a room, or a restaurant table.

New Rule: In a restaurant, a host or partner may rise to greet a new arrival, organize a seat and perhaps pull out the chair. There is no need for others to rise if the new arrival sits down immediately. At a semi-formal gathering when a new person arrives, or anyone leaves, it is normal for all guests to stand for greetings and farewells. This avoids exchanges between a standing and a seated person, which have a way of being embarrassing. Of course, it is perfectly reasonable for someone to remain seated because of a medical problem or simple old age. When someone leaves the room (or a restaurant table) for a short time during the evening it is not necessary for anyone to rise.

Old Rule: A man walks on the outside of a woman while on a pavement, i.e. on the traffic side.

New Rule: There isn't one. Many young people don't even know there ever was a rule.

Introducing People

There are formal rules about introducing people, and there are times when it's obviously your job to perform careful introductions. More generally, in social or work situations if there's the slightest doubt that people know who others are, then you should try to perform simple introductions. If you, with a friend, meet another friend in the street, then if you've stopped, for even a second, you must say, 'This is Jane, this is John.' Of course, you can say lots more if you want, you can also be walking straight on if you want, but you must do it. It is dreadfully bad manners to leave your friends hanging around on the outskirts of a conversation without even a name.

It's even more important at social events. So many otherwise very polite and reasonable people fall down badly on introductions: they think it's not their job, or they're too shy or they think everyone else knows each other already, or they think it's too formal or structured to have name recitals. But introductions are so vital for the proper running of conversations that it doesn't matter who does them. I've probably introduced brothers and sisters to each other before now but *it's better to over-introduce than to under-introduce: don't assume people all know each other*. This is actually another example of not under-estimating your own importance: at a social event you may feel you know hardly anyone, but everyone else might know even fewer people: you may be a link between two groups and you have a duty to mix them.

Thank Yous

What could be more important? When I tell people that I'm writing an etiquette book this, more than any other, is the topic they want me to deal with. They're all horrified by the extent to which other people don't bother to say 'Thank you'. This feeling is so nearly universal that it's hard to make out exactly who are the people who don't thank . . . unless, is it just possible, people are better at expecting it from other people, and noting its absence, than they themselves are at actually remembering to make their 'thank yous'?

It's one of those areas where there is enormous variation, and you have to consider local customs. But, in general, you must thank people properly for everything: for an invitation (even one you're turning down), for a present, for a weekend at their house. You thank them at the time, and if the favour or present was big enough you thank them again later either by letter or in person or over the phone. (A point worth remembering is that if you are thanking a family or group of people, a written thank you can be passed around, while a phone message may not reach everyone concerned.) In some circumstances, you may like to give a small token gift. Don't ever think, 'Oh, they must know how grateful I am, no need to spell it out,' or 'I received so many wedding presents I can't possibly be expected to write to everyone.' Wrong in both cases. I can also tell you that you are unlikely ever to go wrong or offend people by thanking them, but you can easily err by neglecting this little politeness.

Personal Habits
The general consensus is that some mannerisms and habits are unappealing and you should respect that, even if you yourself can't see the point and don't care what others do. The rules include:

1.   Always cover your mouth when coughing or yawning.

2.   Use a handkerchief if you sneeze, or cover your nose with your hand if you have no time to do anything else. Don't pick your nose or sniff.

3.   Beware of scratching yourself or picking at your nails, for example – these things look very unattractive.

In general, the idea is that you shouldn't do things that are unpleasant for other people to be forced to watch.

Clothes
Lots of people dress a certain way and never worry about it, wearing jeans and a shirt to everything from work to a wedding. Many others are unwilling to leave the bedroom unless wearing full make-up and high heels. Those people presumably don't have many problems deciding what to wear. The rest of us (this probably applies more to women than men: men tend to have fewer options of types of outfits, and so fewer ways to go wrong) know whether it's something we're going to worry about. If it is, then take action, or spend time thinking.

If you are going to a very formal function, there will probably be guidelines on the invitation or you can ring the organizers and ask – this is perfectly normal and reasonable. At a less formal event, the best idea is to ask the hostess or another guest. If you're going away on a visit to somewhere smart, it is correct to ask your host (or your friend if he is taking you to stay with his parents): 'Will we be changing for dinner?' A smart dress will take a woman through most events, but this is the one area where men have a harder life, since dinner jackets may be expected at very up-market dinners. This would usually be specified to you at some stage, but there's never any harm in checking.

Fig. 2. Formal attire for a man – dinner jacket, also known as black tie.

If you really can't find out what the correct clothes for an event are, then ask yourself: 'How would I most mind being wrongly dressed?' Some people hate being under-dressed, some find it worse to be too formal, it could be your dream or your nightmare to find yourself wearing more or less the same as everyone else. Use your thoughts on this to choose your outfit: you might still not be dressed perfectly, but you won't have descended to the level of your worst nightmare. We all have dreadful memories of some terrible occasion in the wrong clothes, but try not to worry – it'll make a good story afterwards. And it's surprising how often you find out later that (1) nobody noticed or (2) everyone thought you were very original or (3) one person thought you had terrific style.

2

INFORMAL SOCIAL OCCASIONS

Going out with Friends

Should always be easy and trouble-free, the kind of situation where you don't need etiquette and rules. Unfortunately, this is not always the case. However, things mostly go right, so here I'll only deal with the areas where the problems might come. There is, of course, a sliding scale of formality:

Meeting Friends at a Pub or Wine Bar

You can: turn up late, leave early, wear whatever you like, (probably) bring someone extra along.

Going out for a Group Meal

The limits are narrowed. You should warn someone if you are going to be late or are bringing an extra or can't come after all (though it is perfectly reasonable to do all these things without too much apology). You can wear what you like, provided you have not been asked to dress up for a smart restaurant.

Cinema or Theatre Trip

You can leave early but you'd better not be late. Don't bring an extra unless you've organized the trip/know that tickets won't be bought until you arrive. You can wear what you like. You should have a clear idea of what you want to do afterwards: you may want to go on with the rest of the group to a pub or restaurant, but this is not essential if you'd rather go home.

If one person has bought the tickets, be sure you remember to pay him. If you didn't turn up when a ticket had already been purchased for you, then you must, of course, still pay up. If you are the one who bought the tickets, then don't be shy about asking for payment: people do just forget, and it is perfectly OK to say loudly and clearly, 'Who hasn't paid me yet, then?'

Going to a Friend's House to Watch a Video/Play Cards, etc

Don't be late or bring a friend without checking first. Don't smoke unless your hostess says you can. Even with a good friend living in a squat, watch those manners your mother told you about: don't put a wet glass or hot mug down on a wooden surface without asking if it's OK and don't put your feet up on the furniture unless you ask first, and then take off your shoes. It's the height of rudeness to imply that someone else's furniture is not worthy of respect. (Dinner at a friend's house is dealt with under Attending Dinner Parties, page 54.)

Dropping in on a Friend

You may do this without ringing first *only* if you are willing to be turned away and you give your friend the option of doing this. You can hardly take it amiss if your friend invites you in but carries on watching a favourite TV programme. One point: if you are an unexpected guest you may see something unexpected – from an unlikely lover to a hitherto unmentioned home gym. It is obvious basic politeness to pretend you haven't noticed and not to gossip about it afterwards. And it would be very rude to pass endless comment on things you weren't asked to see (general mess or unwashed dishes, for example), criticize the arrangements ('What, only powdered milk for the coffee!') or poke round in the papers on the table and say, 'What's this then? Who is this from? Is this your phone bill? Let me see how much it is.' If you don't give people the chance to prepare, you can at least be polite about it.

Sorting out the Money

Casual social events – in theory so informal, so stress-free – can be the worst for causing money trouble. There are etiquette rules, and kind rules, and honest rules, but unfortunately huge numbers of people don't bother to stick to any of them. You should know that: (1) no-one is less popular than a person who constantly makes a fuss about money; (2) everyone nourishes the belief that her costs were less than those of everyone else in the group.

Fig. 3. Never comment on what you have seen.

In Pubs and Wine Bars

You may feel that your drink is less expensive than others' so why should you buy a round? First, check this is actually true: soft drinks, for example, are very expensive. If you're sure, then you have two options:

1. Say right from the beginning, 'I'm going to buy my own drinks for tonight, OK? I'm skint and I've just got exactly enough for what I'm having,' or else say you'll be only staying for one drink – people who say that nearly always do stay on so no-one will be surprised. But if you really want to start on this, make sure you stick to it. It's

surprising how many people 'insist' on doing this, then somehow allow some generous soul to include them in his round. It may be just the odd drink but when you've made such a fuss, it looks terribly grasping (probably because it *is* terribly grasping behaviour).

2.   You can find another soul who you think is in a similar situation and suggest that the two of you share rounds – it's a brave person who actually says, 'Why are you two sharing a round and not buying one each?'

You don't have to tip the bar staff, but they take it very kindly if you do. If one has been friendly and helpful all evening, then it is nice to give a small tip at some point – you don't need to keep tipping all evening. If you are lucky enough to drink somewhere with staff who wait on you, then you should certainly tip your waitress if she has managed to keep you happy all evening without too many spilled tomato juices and wrong orders.

Females
In a mixed group you must avoid two kinds of behaviour:

1.   Asking men to go to the bar for you. This is just about acceptable in women over 50, but is very bad form in anyone younger. Going to the bar is a pain, and that is why everyone takes it in turns.

2.   If you are with your boyfriend in a larger group, and you think it is his job to buy your drinks for the evening, this does not mean that the two of you count as one unit for rounds purposes. You must buy one each. It is shaming how many women have a strange lack of understanding of the mathematics of this but it is quite simple. In a group of four, only three of whom are buying rounds, the fourth person can make quite a profit on the evening. Believe me, dear, the other two are noticing, and they are not thinking very much of it.

In Restaurants
The great unresolvable question is whether bills should be split equally. In theory, splitting should work out well: it saves time and worry, and if those present are in vaguely comparable

financial circumstances and all consume at roughly the same rate, then it will be fair. If the group eats out together regularly, then it might be that disparities even out after time. But that isn't always the case. If you are eating out with people much richer than you, you could be worried about getting into something you really can't afford. It's also incredibly annoying if you have carefully chosen the cheapest dishes on the menu and then have to subsidize some hearty man who had two main courses, or if you don't drink much and the table has been ordering bottles of wine all evening followed by a round of liqueurs.

In general: don't suggest splitting the bill unless you're sure of what you're doing. It's easy to think it's fair when it isn't. For example, at Italian restaurants it's quite common for half the group to choose pizza, while the others have a starter and then a meat dish: the disparity in cost can be quite considerable, and the pizza-eaters shouldn't have to pay for the others.

You may think the differences are only small, but it's not really for you to say, is it? You don't know what financial restraints someone else might be under. A quite common scenario is a group from the same office who eat out together for a birthday or celebration: some over-paid managerial type calls for the bill to be split, forgetting that the secretaries earn half what he earns, another colleague ate next to nothing because of her diet, and two others have just taken on huge mortgages.

On the other hand, just like in pubs, there are two warnings for people who think they always cost the least:

1. Fussing over money always looks unattractive. If you want to make the point or insist on paying only your own share, then do it discreetly. Don't get righteous about it and don't go on about it. The best thing is to get someone else on your side, or (rather hypocritically) to appear to be more concerned for other people than for yourself.

2. Don't be so sure all the time that you're being cheated quite as much as you think. A very unpopular person (nearly always a woman) is the one who says, 'I just had soup and a roll and that comes to £5 and here it is,' and somehow forgets the one drink before and the coffee afterwards, and who leaves everyone else to pay the tip. Bills just *are* always bigger than you're expecting, and you

shouldn't always assume that it's nothing to do with you. You may be quite surprised what you've forgotten. (Shared side-dishes? Bread which they charge for? A cover charge?) And again, people who say, 'Oh, I'm not drinking tonight,' will often take just half a glass from the communal bottle, as well as ordering those expensive soft drinks. Vegetarians are particularly prone to assuming their meals are much less expensive than all those meat-laden plates: this is by no means always true. (Quite likely soft drinks and vegetarian food *should* be less expensive, but it's not your friends' fault if they aren't.)

Tipping in Restaurants
This is troublesome because there is no general agreement as to what a tip represents, let alone how much it should be. Restaurant staff will say it's part of their pay. Most customers think it should be dependent on good service. Whatever, if you want to tip, ten per cent of the bill is the minimum to aim for. There are two particular problems: bad service and groups.

I think the service has to be very bad, or outrageously slow, before you leave no tip at all. A reduced tip is another possibility. If they made a mistake and then tried to put it right, then it's unfair to leave no tip at all. A mistake that they didn't care about is sufficient reason not to leave a tip. I'd always give staff points (and money) for trying, for being polite and friendly (and, if necessary, apologetic) even if things went wrong.

If you don't leave a tip, then you could tell someone in authority why you haven't. I must say that I've never got very far with this (suggesting that bad management has been trickling down) but, on principle, you should give people the opportunity to put things right – for future customers, even if it's too late for you. Don't be intimidated. You are the customer, you have the options, and you need never come back.

In a group visit to a restaurant you may find that your companions have completely different ideas as to what constitutes a tip. (This is why many restaurants automatically add a service charge to the bills of large parties.) You just have to give what you think is right yourself and hope others will agree. If the bill is being shared evenly, then it's easy to suggest that each person puts in a certain sum and say, 'That pays the bill and leaves a reasonable tip' – most people are quite happy with that.

Good Behaviour in Pubs and Restaurants

Males (and females too, but much more commonly men) should watch the following points:

1. Never push people to drink more than they want. It is dreadful bad manners and can be dangerous. There are lots of reasons why people may not want to drink (for instance, they've seen what it does to you!) and they are not at all obliged to tell you them. (If you are faced with this kind of behaviour, you just must be firm and unapologetic. You shouldn't need to give any excuse, but if you feel happier just say, 'I'm driving,' or 'I have health reasons for not drinking.') Spiking someone's drink is completely beyond the pale, not even remotely funny, and, of course, very, very dangerous – he may be intending to drive, or may possibly be taking a drug which is fatal when mixed with alcohol, or could be a reformed alcoholic to whom even a drop might be disastrous.

2. Don't harass the staff in pubs and restaurants. Again, dreadful bad manners. You may have only the best intentions towards your waitress, you may feel you are indulging in a little harmless flirtation. She may keep smiling at you. But you should remember that she may well feel that she cannot do anything else: she may be frightened of losing her job, she probably can't tip your salad over your head if she doesn't like the way you behave to her, and she may not be sure of getting backing from the management if she complains. If your attentions are unwelcome to a friend or stranger or fellow customer, she does have the option of walking out or being rude. Try to imagine what it must be like if you can't do that, if you feel you just have to stand there and take it.

3

FORMAL MEALS

Basic Table Manners

The Fork Question
It would be nice to think that by now nobody cares about the old 'Which fork?' question, but I expect that's optimistic. The first thing to stress is that it doesn't matter all that much if you get it wrong. In a restaurant, if you find yourself with the wrong eating irons, you call over your waiter and say, 'Could you bring me another fork, please?' In someone's house you could ask politely for more supplies, or use the same fork for the first course – you will have been given enough cutlery for the food, so if you use the wrong one there must be something left over which you use next time round.

If you want to get it right, then remember that you start from the outside and work your way in. Surrounding your plate (or the area where your plate will be) is a variety of items of cutlery: look at the outside edges to see what to use next. Use your imagination of course: if it's a spoon and your dish is pâté, then look for a knife. Use what you'd use at home.

In a restaurant whoever laid the table may not have known what you were going to eat. After you have ordered, a waiter may come round and say, 'Who was having the fish? Eggs? Pâté? Steak?' and he will change the cutlery accordingly. This is your chance to learn which items are needed for which dishes. Cutlery for later courses may be brought with the food, so don't panic if you don't seem to have enough spoons.

Other Cutlery Difficulties
If you have a selection of knives on your right-hand side, the smallest will be your bread-and-butter knife, which you move to

Fig. 4. A formal place setting.

the side plate on your left-hand side. (It may already be there.) If they're all the same size, it doesn't matter which you use.

There is a right and wrong way to hold knives and forks: you should end up with your first finger pointing away from you along the piece of cutlery. This is difficult to visualize and much the best way, if you're not sure, is to eye covertly someone whose table manners you respect and copy them. You hold the fork so that the back of it (the side which is normally touching the table top, the convex curve) is towards you. This means that food may be speared on the points, or balanced on the back of the fork, but you may not, traditionally, turn the fork over and use it as you would a spoon or scoop. (See Fig. 5 overleaf.) However, rules on eating have loosened up and few will frown nowadays if, for example, you use the American system and eat mostly using your fork in your right hand.

At the end of a meal you should place knife and fork together, half-way across the plate – a six o'clock position. For other courses, the rules aren't so clear. If, for example, a soup or pudding is served on a plate you can leave the cutlery on either bowl or plate. Use your common sense: if the bowl is tiny and likely to tip over, then put the spoon on the plate. Just make sure it looks reasonably neat, and that if you used two implements they are tidily together.

Politeness During the Meal
You don't start eating until everyone else at your table has been served and/or your host begins eating. This still holds good in a

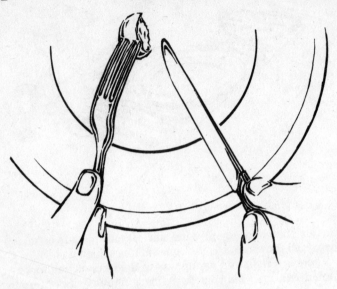

Fig. 5. Holding a knife and fork.

private home (unless your host says, 'Do start'). In a restaurant if everyone is being served at the same time, you hold back until all the waiters have left. But if, as is often the case, starters or puddings are being brought fairly haphazardly, it is polite to say, 'I'll start this if no-one minds,' if the item is hot and sizzling or ice-cream is in danger of melting.

Finishing up soup, you tilt the bowl away from you. You don't make slurping noises while drinking it.

Keep your elbows off the table in formal company and during the early part of a meal – this isn't too dreadful a crime these days, and among friends or during an intimate chat it is fine. The older generation may still raise their eyebrows although almost everyone relaxes about it as a meal wears on. Between courses and during coffee it is all right.

Never talk with your mouth full; it is very bad manners and incredibly unattractive to look at. It's embarrassing to be asked a question just as you've taken a mouthful, but still better to mumble a closed-mouth 'Excuse me' and chew on than try to answer and eat at the same time.

If a mouthful contains something inedible (for example, pips or bones), then you *discreetly* remove it. The best way is in your clenched fist: spit the item into your hand and the whole thing can be passed off as a cough. You may also use your napkin or – at a pinch – your spoon or fork. The bone or stone can then be placed on the side of your plate. If a mouthful is so burning hot you feel you can't swallow it, then again you must try to be as discreet as possible, using hands and napkin to hide the unappetizing sight of your spitting it out.

(See also section on Difficult Foods on page 39.)

Eating in Grand Restaurants

There is one very important point here. No matter how grand, expensive or pretentious the restaurant, you are the customer. They are there for your benefit, to serve you, and you (or your companion) are paying a lot of money for that. So you should not be intimidated.

A really good restaurant should make life pleasant for you, not difficult, and adapt to your every whim. At a fast-food joint you have to decide what you want from a strange list written over your head with unhelpful pictures, shout it at the operative, struggle with your money, find yourself somewhere to sit and then unwrap your food to eat it. A grand restaurant should make eating a lot easier than this, not harder. Relax and enjoy.

Unfortunately, there are expensive restaurants where the staff are not friendly and helpful, but sneering and rude. There are waiters who will try to make you feel stupid and small if you make a mistake or don't understand something. But be absolutely clear: if this is the case, then this is *not* a good restaurant. If it is one member of staff, then you should complain. If it is the whole ethos of the place, then don't go there again. It really is that simple. No waiter ever should correct your pronunciation, sigh, become impatient or give you unwanted advice or corrections.

So, normally, visiting a grand place should be a pleasure. But we have to accept that you may have gone into the wrong sort of restaurant by accident and, of course, you'll never go there again, but you're stuck with it now and you don't want to be so fazed by the waiters that it wrecks your enjoyment of this expensive meal. The other possibility is that you fear your companion is ready to despise your lack of poise, or at the very least is going to be rather surprised after you exaggerated your knowledge of French and implied you came to this kind of place every week.

There are two golden rules to remember:

1.   Always ask, and risk a momentary embarrassment, rather than end up with something you didn't really want, or don't know what to do with.

2.   Even among the very grandest establishments there are huge variations in the way food is served, what items are called, the number and order of courses. Even if you eat out expensively every night you would still constantly find new customs and rituals and ways of doing things in different restaurants. So don't be embarrassed about not knowing or realizing something – it doesn't mark you down as a new kid (and it wouldn't matter a bit if it did).

Clothes

Dress up all you want, but don't worry too much – who sees what you're wearing when you're sitting at a table anyway? Some restaurants have minimum standards: no jeans and training shoes, and they expect men to wear a shirt and jacket, and occasionally a tie. So it's better to err on the safe side or carry a tie in your pocket if you don't normally wear one.

What to Do When You Get There

All you should have to do is get yourself through the door. Beyond this point the staff will tell you where to go and when. Someone should come to greet you: one of you should give your name (or ask for the person you are meeting) and the reservation time. A waiter will take your coats, and then usually show you to a seating area and offer to get you drinks (although you can ask to go straight to your table). You will be given menus to look at. Often a plate of snacks will be offered to you. These are free (well, you pay for them somehow, but they won't appear on the bill). They are sometimes known as *amuse-gueule* and may include small sample items from the list of starters (if you can match them up with the description on the menu, then you'll have extra help in choosing). The waiter takes your order when you're ready: if you need more time to choose, then ask him to come back in a few minutes.

You will eventually be taken to your table by a waiter, who

may pull out your chair for you and place your napkin in your lap (particularly if you're a woman).

The Menu

In Great Britain the menu won't normally be in French, though it may include French words. There is no need to be embarrassed if you don't know what something means: ask your companion (no matter how exalted) or the waiter. You can ask the waiter about several different dishes if you like. Don't think that if he has just described something at length you must have it. It is perfectly reasonable to ask if a dish contains some ingredient you particularly like or dislike. I should warn you that some-times this information would have been crystal-clear to someone else, but you shouldn't let that bother you. Some descriptive words imply that a particular food is present: for example, 'Florentine' in the name of a dish usually means spinach. But Florentine is also the name of a chocolate biscuit/cake, and beefsteak Florentine does not contain spinach, so don't let anyone put you down for asking. They shouldn't, I'm just warning you.

In general, anyone being paid for in a restaurant should choose from the same price range as the host, unless the host clearly (and *convincingly*) says, 'I'm having simple food because I'm on a diet, but I'd like you to have whatever you want.' There are still a few places where a woman dining with a man is given a menu without any prices on it – for example in some London clubs only the member is given a priced menu. I think this is one custom which should be abolished immediately, but you might just come across it, so you'll need to use your common sense.

Roughly speaking, remember this:

STARTERS

Cheap:	Melon, grapefruit, soup.
Medium:	Anything meat- or fish-based such as pâté, seafood.
Expensive:	Smoked salmon, oysters, snails, caviare.

MAIN COURSES

Cheap:	Most fish, offal (liver, kidneys), vegetarian food, anything like seafood pancakes.
Medium:	Chicken, salmon, lamb cutlets, game.

| Expensive: | Steaks. |
| Very expensive: | Lobster. |

Table d'hôte

If you select whatever dishes you want from the normal, full menu you are choosing *à la carte*. The other option is choosing the *table d'hôte*: this offers a smaller selection, normally three or four courses, at a set price, or a price based on your choice of main course. If your restaurant offers this option, you can normally find it listed on one loose page clipped to your menu. If your companion chooses from the *table d'hôte*, and is paying, it is mannerly to do the same. It can mean a quite substantial saving, and also means that you have a clear idea of how much the meal costs right from the beginning as the *table d'hôte* will include the potatoes and vegetables, and possibly also the coffee. It will certainly be clearly stated what it does include. If you are at all panicked by the thought of finding your way round an enormous and complicated menu, then choosing the *table d'hôte* makes life much easier.

The Courses

A smart restaurant meal could consist of quite a lot of courses: soup, starter, fish, sorbet, meat course, pudding, cheese, coffee.

In practice nowadays there will usually be only four main groups of food for you to choose from:

STARTERS

With soup as one option.

MAIN COURSES

Which could be described on the menu as *entrées*. (*Entrée* – nowadays – is just another word for main course. It tends to imply a made-up dish – rather than a steak or a slice off the roast – but not necessarily. People use all these terms very freely these days, so don't worry.) *Entrées* will include fish and meat dishes. If you have vegetables and potatoes, the waiter will bring these round and serve you from dishes containing portions for all your party. He will expect some guidance from you as to what you want. If you can't tell what something in the dish is, then ask. You should, of course, bear in mind how many more of

your party the dish has to go round, but on the whole that's the
waiter's problem, not yours.

PUDDING

Many restaurants now provide a sweet trolley to be trundled
over to your table. The waiter should describe each item briefly.
If you want a reminder when your turn comes, or more detail,
ask away. If you'd like a little bit of more than one pudding,
then ask for that. A friendly waiter may give you a tiny portion
to try, but you still don't have to choose that one. You will be
given a spoon and fork to eat it with: you are intended to use the
fork to push the food onto the spoon. However, if you want to
use only the spoon, or only the fork, then that's OK.

CHEESE

Is generally an alternative to pudding. The waiter will bring the
cheese board and biscuits over and wait for you to say what you
want. He should name all the cheeses, and you can ask him to
repeat them if you like. You don't have to say the names of the
ones you want, just point and say, 'That one.' Don't be intimidated into choosing only one cheese or the wrong kind of
biscuits: ask for exactly what you want. They don't actually
mind how many (or how large) chunks you have and, even if
they did, it's not their business to mind.

EXTRAS

You may be offered a sorbet (a water-ice) between courses to
clear the palate, or a savoury at the end of the meal – something
like egg and anchovy on toast (called Scotch woodcock) or
bacon wrapped round oysters (angels on horseback). As neither
of these courses (whatever the restaurant concerned may pretend) is either usual or obligatory these days, it is up to the
waiters to tell you what is happening and what the dish consists
of. Do not be nervous about asking.

Wines

If you know what you're doing and know your budget, fine.
Otherwise: quite honestly an expensive restaurant is not the
place to experiment with wine. If you want to try something
really good, then you're much better off buying it from your
off-licence and having it at home. It will be half the price or less,
and that is a promise.

There is nothing wrong with having the house wine – at a good restaurant it should be good, and, if it isn't, what makes you think their more expensive selections will be any better? One thing: if someone is taking you out to eat and you think he may be slightly nervous about the cost, it would be good, tactful manners to say, 'I always think the house wine is fine, don't you? I'm perfectly happy with that, if you are.' Your escort may have been too nervous to say this for fear of appearing mean. If you are paying, then you should have no qualms about suggesting the house wine, if that is what suits your pockets and inclinations. If your companion looks surprised (very bad manners), then I suggest you claim that a wine guide/glossy magazine/close friend who is a wine master has told you that the house wine here is superb.

Traditionally, red wine goes with red meat, white wine goes with chicken or fish. Don't feel bound by that, though – if you're not heavy drinkers you could have a problem if two of you order different main courses. Have whatever you like the sound of. Some wine lists are very helpful on this. So are some wine waiters, but unfortunately many of them don't really seem to understand the words 'and not too expensive' in the way you mean them. What they can do is tell you if a wine is sweet or dry, or if it's heavy or strong-tasting. Never let a wine waiter choose for you unless you are willing to spend a lot of money. Even if the partner of your dreams has just agreed to marry you, do not call for a 'bottle of champagne'. Ask for the wine list and check the price, or you may find you've spent your entire wedding budget already.

If you're intending to dilute white wine with mineral water, then it's simply not worth choosing a really good expensive wine. If you want water, then state clearly whether you mean ordinary water or mineral water. Don't be intimidated into paying for Perrier if all you want is tap water.

Tasting

If you choose house wine, it is not normally offered for tasting.

If you choose from the full list, the waiter will show the bottle to the host of the party, who should check that what's written on the label is what he remembers ordering. The waiter opens the bottle and pours a little for the host, who swills it round in the glass, sniffs it, takes a sip, and nods if it's all right. The waiter then pours out for the rest of the party, serving women first and finishing filling the host's glass last.

The wine waiter should treat as host the person who ordered the wine, and, of course, this is not necessarily a man. The technical host might also suggest that someone else (a guest who is more expert perhaps) should do the tasting – all that is necessary is to so indicate to the wine waiter.

If you are tasting and think it's not quite right, then the easiest thing is to ask for a second opinion from another guest. If he agrees, politely ask for the bottle to be changed. The restaurant should be ready to do so, even if they think there's nothing wrong with it.

Difficult Foods

In the film *Pretty Woman* the heroine doesn't know how to eat snails and they jump off the plate, to be caught by a perfect waiter. He says, 'It happens all the time,' which shows that it really is a good restaurant.

It is not at all difficult to eat snails once you've got the hang of it, but don't pretend you've had them before if you haven't, as it will be hard to hide that you are learning as you eat. You will probably be given a pair of strange tongs and a very small fork or spear-like instrument. The idea is that you hold the snail shell in the tongs in your left hand, and use the little pick to pull out the meat. Swizzle the little chunk of meat round in the sauce in the bottom of the dish, then pop it (still on the pick) whole into your mouth. When you've eaten all the snails, you can eat the rest of your sauce with a spoon, or mop it up with bread. This may sound rather un-grand, but that's the way to do it. That sauce, by the way, is composed mostly of butter and garlic, which may be a reason for not ordering snails in some situations.

Mussels are quite similar: they are normally served in their shells and you pick one up in your fingers and use either a teaspoon or – very French and chic – the empty shell from the first mussel as pincers to scoop the soft bit out and carry it whole to your mouth. Again, any remaining liquid at the bottom of the dish should be eaten with your spoon. With both snails and mussels, you are normally given an extra plate or bowl for the debris, i.e. empty shells.

These are both dishes to enjoy, but they are not honestly very dignified to eat, so only order them if you're going to make the most of them and not be worrying about what your companion thinks or if you've got a splash of something on your nose.

Fig. 6. Eating snails, mussels and globe artichokes.

Globe artichokes are usually served with a dish of hollandaise sauce. With your fingers you tear off a leaf at a time, dip the broad fleshy part into the sauce and eat this half, discarding the rest of the leaf. When you reach the centre of the artichoke, scrape off the fuzzy bits with a fork, then eat the soft central 'heart' with knife and fork. This isn't as difficult as it all sounds, just complicated. Ask or watch if it's your first time and it will become obvious.

Finger-bowls

A finger-bowl is normally a wide, shallow bowl (about the diameter of a saucer) which may have a few leaves, or flowers, or a slice of lemon floating on top. Any water for drinking would undoubtedly be served in something you would immediately recognize as a glass. A finger-bowl is a sign that whatever it is you are about to eat may safely be eaten with the fingers, so it should be treated as a useful clue, not a threat. In case its purpose is not apparent, it's for you to wash your dirty fingers in after eating your corn on the cob or whatever. You may be supplied with a second napkin, or you may dry your hands on the one you already have.

Finger Foods
Spare ribs, mussels and so on are items you're expected to eat with your fingers. Unfortunately, with most meat dishes on the bone you are not expected to pick up and chew, even if you do feel that the very best bits of your cutlets or game-bird are impossible to reach by fork. Of course, there's nothing to stop you doing it if you're feeling brave, but if you're trying to be super-correct then you ought not to. Men will get away with it more easily than women if you do want to try it. (In less grand restaurants, or at someone's house, you have to judge the situation: if others are doing it, fine, or if the occasion is informal enough for you to say, 'No-one minds if I pick this up, do they?' – you may even find others grateful to you for taking the lead – then go ahead. At a dinner party you can say it's because it's so delicious you must get every scrap, so passing it off as a compliment to the cook.)

Hot Towels
Until recently these were found only on aeroplanes and in Chinese restaurants, but they are turning up elsewhere these days. Towels is a misnomer – they're actually hot damp face-cloths. Your waiter would probably drop one on the plate in front of you with tongs: it is usually rolled up and resembles a sausage roll in size and shape. You pick it up, shake it out (saying, 'Ow ow ow', because it really is hot) and wipe it over your hands. The heat disperses very quickly, and your hands dry almost immediately, and the whole effect is very refreshing. (If you want to have a quick dab at your mouth and chin, then that's fine too – just be discreet, and careful if you're wearing lipstick.) Put the crumpled item back on your plate and the waiter will remove it.

Variations in Customs

One thing to remember about visiting grand restaurants is that customs vary not only within a country, but widely from one part of the world to the next. You probably wouldn't feel embarrassed about not being too sure what to do in a Chinese or Japanese restaurant – whether grand or simple – and would happily ask your waiter or companion for advice. There is no reason why you should feel differently about a British or quasi-French restaurant.

Tipping

Smart restaurants are very used to this and will do their very best to make it easy for you. Everything about tipping in cheaper eateries applies here. Expect to add at least ten per cent, and more like fifteen per cent may be half-expected. Don't worry about dividing it among the different levels of staff you've encountered: leave the tip on the plate (or at the bottom of the credit card bill) and they will divvy it up how they want. If there is a cloakroom attendant, you would expect to leave a small tip there. Women being taken out and paid for by men often bring nothing in their evening bag and get embarrassed in the cloak-room, either because their escort isn't there to ask, or else they find it difficult to ask directly for cash. It's worth trying to remember to bring at least a handful of change, no matter how tiny the bag and generous the companion.

Mistakes

1.   You place your order and the waiter says, 'Madam has ordered three starters and no main course.' If those are the dishes you actually want, then say, 'Yes, that is what I'd like. Please serve the soup with the other starters, and the other two dishes afterwards.' Any restaurant should be able to cope with this. If it was a mistake on your part say, 'I must have misunderstood the menu. Please take the others' orders while I look again,' and re-choose from the menu. Try to stay calm, take as much time as you want, and don't be panicked into ordering the first thing you can see that obviously is a main course.

2.   If you spill something, the waiter will deal with it. If your own clothes are threatened, then head straight for the rest

rooms to dab or sponge. Salt is famously good for red wine stains, so apply this at the table first. If there's one thing restaurants are used to it's spills, and they should be able to cope and help you too.

Unfortunately, the world seems to divide into two camps on this: half of them think restaurant staff are automatons, paid to do dirty jobs like clearing up after messy customers. The customer is paying, so there is no need whatsoever to apologize, explain or thank, or do anything except sigh with irritation if they feel the clearer-up is taking too long and is in the way. The other half of humanity apologizes manically as if they had broken the owner's family heirlooms. Neither side is right. It's obviously polite to thank anyone who helps you, and say sorry to someone who has to get down on his hands and knees to scrub the floor, but there is no need for the profuse apologies and regrets and offers to make amends you would produce if you had done this in someone's private home (unless you have done a phenomenal amount of damage – the restaurant should be insured, but it would be nice to check and to offer extra apologies). If the restaurant coped particularly well, you might like to reflect this in the tip, and even perhaps say, 'Some of this is for whoever has to clear up the mess.'

4

FORMAL FUNCTIONS

Specially Grand Dinners
You may get invited to a banquet or to eat at some other formal
function – for example, a feast or High Table meal at an
Oxbridge college. This is similar to a smart restaurant, but
simpler in that you probably don't get any choice of food. You
will be surrounded by other people (guests are usually crammed
together along long tables at this kind of thing, so it's quite an
intimate atmosphere) and it should be easy to watch others if
you have any doubts about where you're up to in the cutlery or
what exactly you're supposed to be doing with whatever this is
on your plate.

Getting Seated
There will usually be a table plan outside the banqueting hall or
dining room so you can check where you're due to sit, and get a
quick fix on who's sitting next to you (not necessarily your
partner, if you have one). Make your way to this seat when told
to: there will be a place card, you're not expected to carry the
table plan in your head. There will probably also be a menu card,
listing all the dishes and the wines. You can then prepare
yourself mentally for what's coming and whether you're going to
like it. Your place will be laid as at a restaurant, with several
glasses in front of you. That needn't worry you; it's up to the
servers to make sure you get the right liquid in the right
receptacle.

The first difference from a restaurant is that you don't have
your friendly waiter as such and the serving staff are usually in a
terrific hurry, so you may have to solve more of your own
problems. Don't worry though – the sheer numbers of people at

a large function means that it won't matter if you do slightly the wrong thing because no-one will notice. If you do use the wrong fork, then you might not be able to get an easy replacement, but don't panic. There will be plenty of cutlery on the table. If you use your main course fork for your starter, say, you have two easy options: use your starter fork for your meat (no-one will notice) or discreetly hang on to the large fork, surreptitiously lick it clean, and use it again. Easy.

Serving Yourself

The one really big deal about this kind of dinner can be serving yourself. This is horrendous for the uninitiated: a white-gloved operative appears over your left shoulder with a huge plate of slices of meat. You suddenly realize that he isn't going to serve you. He (and, it seems, the whole table) is waiting for you to serve yourself. It is really no more difficult to do than to help yourself from a dish at home, but it feels it. The operative is (we hope) used to this and will hold the dish firmly and at a helpful angle, though this may seem rather high. If it is not clear how much of the dish you are meant to take, then you simply ask. This (I have it on the highest authority) is what you are meant and expected to do. If you listen carefully at Oxbridge High Tables you will probably hear the querulous voice of some old don saying, 'Can I really have only one quail, Benson?' to some aged college employee, or the cold tones of a waiter saying, 'I believe, sir, that the correct portion is one.' And remember, no-one is watching you, waiting for you to make a fool of yourself. When you have gone through this (admittedly nerve-racking) ritual once, you will never be quite so worried again. It is mercifully rare, of course, and nearly everywhere serves your food out to you nowadays. But if you know it's coming you can at least watch the progress of the food up the table and see what others are doing – unless of course, as once happened to me, you turn out to be senior lady guest present, and everything gets offered to you first. I think that was a piece of bad luck.

Conversation

As mentioned before, you may be separated from your partner. I once said, late on, to my escort at a very formal dinner, 'Gosh, I haven't spoken to you all evening.' 'That's as it should be,' he said approvingly. You must make an effort to talk to those on either side of you. Strict rules – talking to your left for the first two courses and then turning to your right for the rest – are more or less gone now and conversation can be very general, across and along the table. It's polite, of course, just to keep checking that neither of your neighbours is sitting in silence. If you want to strike up with your neighbour or anyone else, you simply ask the usual questions: 'I'm X, who are you? . . . What do you do? Where do you live?'

You may be asked formally to drink the health of the Queen. When the Loyal Toast is called, you hold up your glass and murmur, 'The Queen'. At the end of the meal, port may be passed. It travels clockwise, which in practice means that it will arrive from your right and must be passed to your left. It's everyone's job to keep the bottle or decanter on the move – you have to keep remembering to watch out or ask your neighbour to nudge you.

I have been at a formal dinner where after pudding but before dessert (the word is used freely nowadays but technically refers to fruit, nuts and port after the meal) we were turned out into a nearby garden to wander and chat for a few minutes while the table was cleared. On returning we had each been allotted a new place, with new people to talk to, which was rather a good custom I thought. (I had been sitting next to a very charming Dr A Rogers, and when I came back the same name was apparently still beside me. I was pleased but puzzled, until a very glamorous woman came and sat down – my new friend's wife was equally well qualified.)

Royal Garden Party

An invitation to a garden party at Buckingham Palace in London or the Palace at Holyroodhouse in Edinburgh will contain very full details of what to do, including where to park and how to reach the correct entrance. A letter of acceptance is not necessary (although you may write one if you wish) as the invitation is seen as a Royal command and it is assumed you will attend. A letter of refusal must give a very good reason.

Dress

Most men will wear morning suit (see page 96), uniform or national dress, although lounge suits are acceptable now. Women wear afternoon dress and a hat (although the hat is not obligatory). In effect, guests wear what they would to a formal wedding.

The Royal Family
You must not approach them directly. If any Royal wishes to speak to you, a household aide will approach you and tell you what to do, then formally present you.

Leaving
The party ends at 6 pm with the national anthem. The Royals withdraw to the Palace and guests leave in their own time.

Other Formal Events
Whether it's an embassy reception, a hunt ball or a friend's twenty-first there is one thing to remember: if in doubt, ask. It's impossible to lay down rules which will cover all events, but the organizers of almost all functions will be glad to help you with any problems (what to wear, when and how to arrive). You ring up and ask them, whether it's a paid office or a friend's mother.

If you think you may be introduced to someone very important, and you know in advance their title, then you can check the table of forms of address on page 159 of this book. But you needn't worry too much – such people are, for a start, used to meeting new people all the time and won't be put off by your nerves or imperfect grasp of the finer points of their titles. You can use 'Sir' or 'Madam' for anyone and it is, anyway, not unspeakably rude to say, 'How do you do?' or 'Thank you for asking me,' and so on without any title at all.

The basics apply at such events as much as anywhere: answer invitations promptly, thank hosts afterwards, be prepared to strike up a conversation with anyone, don't smoke unless you're sure it's OK, remember your table manners, and if in doubt watch what others (well-mannered others . . .) are doing so that you can match them. Oh, and try not to be so nervous that you don't enjoy yourself.

5

GIVING DINNER PARTIES

Smarter Parties

Suppose you are inviting some vital person or couple whom you're desperate to impress, or who you think could have an important effect on your life, and you worry that your normal entertaining style is too casual or informal? Well, you're probably wrong: if that's your style, then you use it for everyone. A key rule for entertaining is *don't ever get too far away from your own normal standards*. You may think that your boss and partner or future in-laws will be horrified by your Bohemian ways, but that's unlikely to be true. They won't be expecting expensive matching china and Waterford crystal (particularly not your boss, who knows how much you earn) and might even find it refreshing to eat in a more relaxed and casual atmosphere than normal.

The host always has the right to dictate the pace and the level of formality: even if your boss normally eats his evening meal with seven courses, seven sets of cutlery and seven kinds of wine, he follows your rules and customs in your house. And if you visited him you wouldn't expect him to say, 'We normally use the Wedgwood dinner service, but as you're here we've got plastic plates instead,' would you? Stick to your guns, and plan your dinner party the way you would if the guests were friends your own age.

Treating your boss as an honoured guest at an informal supper party is fine: the road to disaster lies in pretending you do things differently, panic-buying items you've managed without for years (silver place-card holders, ramekins), and trying out pretentious ideas that you neither like nor would normally give house room to. Of course, there is nothing wrong with liking to give an elaborate dinner with gourmet food and some formality *if that is your style*. I am only warning against pretending to customs that don't come naturally to you.

Paper Napkins and Improvisation

You may not have sufficient quantities of items to eat and drink with, out of and off. None of the following is bad etiquette, whatever some people might tell you: paper napkins, guests using same plates and cutlery for starter and main course, mugs for coffee, same glass for different wines, china, glasses or cutlery which don't match, unequal numbers of men and women, table placing which doesn't alternate men and women exactly.

How to Cope

1. Try to make sure your flat or house is as clean and tidy as possible – you don't want to put people off or make them feel that the food is being produced in dirty surroundings. Even if you don't always use a dining table, try to if you possibly can this time.

2. Don't try to cook something more expensive or elaborate than normal. This is the worst time to try that, as your guests may be people you'd be reluctant to admit failure to. Good honest, cheap food is fine for anyone: meat loaf, pasta dishes, casseroles are ideal for entertaining. (But if you want to do something very spicy, make sure your guests like that, or provide some milder dishes too.) Don't think, 'Older guests – roast,' if you're not used to doing roasts. You'll find they're elaborate, time-consuming and very difficult to get right first time. It's particularly hard to get the timings right for them and they require your presence in the kitchen virtually full-time in the final half-hour. Which brings us on to:

3. Another good reason for cooking something simple is that with these guests you should try specially hard not to spend too much time in the kitchen. You should make sure you'll have plenty of time to welcome them when they arrive, taking their coats and showing them the bathroom and providing drinks. You should not rush off to the kitchen every ten seconds. If there are two of you, then at least one should stay with them and chat and check they're

OK. If you're single you might like to choose a trusted friend as co-host for the evening so one of you can do this. If you have invited same-age friends too, it's polite to make sure your older friends get the comfortable armchairs and the least improvised dining chairs.

4. Make sure you perform proper introductions with any other guests.

5. Have a rough seating plan in your mind. It doesn't matter if you don't plan every placement, but you should decide where you are sitting (generally as near to the kitchen as possible) and then remember that the senior female guest (i.e. your boss or a male boss's wife or your mother-in-law) should sit on the host's right and the senior male guest on the right of the hostess. Again, if you're single choose your most trusted friend to look after the other guest. You can change that round if it suits better – alternating men and women isn't at all essential these days and if you are a woman entertaining single-handed and want your female boss to sit next to you, then fine. If there are four of you, two couples, then you can alternate by gender or else sit the other couple on either side of you. Just make sure you think in advance who will sit where. Place cards would probably look pretentious if they're not your usual style or if there's only a few of you. You simply tell your guests where you'd like them to sit.

6. Keep an eye out to make sure your guests are comfortable. It may be, if they are older than you, that they are not familiar with the food, say, and may in general be more reluctant than your own friends to ask for what they want. Make sure you explain properly what everything is and, if necessary, how to eat it. Make sure they know where the bathroom is. Offer water or fruit juice if they're not drinking alcohol. Remember to provide napkins.

7. If you're particularly nervous about your guests you might like to think in advance of a few topics of conversation. You can always ask what TV programmes they watch, do they read and if so what, do they like films or the theatre? An older couple can usually be brought to talk about their

children very easily, but never imply that an older female guest might only be interested in children or housework: ask her about her job or politics or literature instead.

8. Don't apologize too much. The truth is that most people won't know exactly how you intended the food to be. It is not good manners (and is boring) to go on about the food, wringing your hands and saying, 'I'm sorry it's not very nice.' If you possibly can, make no comment at all about how it turned out, and most people will tell you it's fine. If you have to own up to terrible disasters, try to be light-hearted about it. Most guests won't be at all worried by the problem but will be uncomfortable if you are on the point of tears. No culinary horror ever need spoil a dinner party beyond repair – unless, I suppose, the dinner party was your audition for a job cooking! Just remember, it never is that serious for the guests.

All these things are much more important than whether all the plates match. The same rules apply, in fact, to entertaining your own friends. It's just that an older couple may need a bit more looking after. And remember: make sure there's enough to eat and drink, be polite and pleasant, try to make sure your guests are always comfortable and make sure the conversation swings along. These things demonstrate your good manners far more than starched linen napkins would.

Dinner for Friends
If you're just having friends round to eat, then it's nice to have things as comfortable and pleasant for them as possible, but you are functioning as a kind organizer of a social event, not a paid owner of a restaurant. That's not to say you shouldn't make any effort at all for a supper party. Just make sure people are enjoying themselves. That generally is more important than worrying about the finer points of traditional etiquette.

The section above on smarter parties will give you the general idea: you will know for yourself where you'd like to be less formal with friends.

Food and Drink
Whether you're a gourmet cook or a complete beginner, these are the good manners' requirements:

1.   Make sure there's enough to eat.

2.   Keep it simple enough that you can spend most of your time with your guests, and not out in the kitchen cooking.

VEGETARIANS

In a perfect world, vegetarians would say, on being invited to dinner, 'I'd love to come. Do you know that I don't eat meat?' The Perfect Hostess would say, 'That's fine. I can plan the menu accordingly.'

It is always the polite guest's job to inform the hostess of any special food requirements: but this doesn't always work out, so it may be safer for hostesses to ask.

Hostesses should: try to do something for the veggies, point out clearly which dishes they can't eat, and *don't cheat* by using meat stock or meat fat where you think it won't be noticed. Lots of vegetarians don't like to eat food which has been kept or cooked in the same container as meat. You may think this is affectation, but you should try to respect it. Some vegetarians say they are sick after eating meat-tainted products, so be warned, cheating cooks, you may get caught out.

If an unexpected vegetarian turns up, you'll have to try to improvise: rustle up some bread and cheese, or plain pasta tossed in butter and Parmesan. Try to be reasonably gracious about it – the situation will enhance your reputation as a host who can cope (even if you think your coping was a near thing).

If you cook both vegetarian and meat dishes, the problem can be that your meat-eating friends (manic on the subject normally) will always choose this meal to say, 'Hey, the lentil loaf looks nice.' Now, many veggies think meat-eaters should be encouraged to eat less meat, but that's a general principle and you may be surprised at how quickly it disappears when they see their meal under threat. Veggies are always pleased if there's a few of them at a dinner table ('We practically out-number them!') but they keep a keen eye out for the portions. Be prepared to say, 'Veggies get first choice, meat-eaters hold back,' and enforce it.

Lots of vegetarians eat fish, but some get touchy if asked – 'Why should I/shouldn't I?' come out equally aggressively – or tell you that they'd rather eat wild salmon than battery eggs (wouldn't we all?).

Vegetarian hostesses should not feel obliged to cook meat: it does nobody any harm to refrain from meat for the odd meal. Many people have eaten a delicious meal, complimented and thanked the cook, then been shocked and disgruntled to find there was no meat in it.

Extra Guests

Hostesses have to be firm. If someone says, 'May I bring my new boyfriend/the friend who'll be staying with me that night?' right out, then it is not bad manners to say, 'No,' and that person should be ready for such a reply. If she is not, then it is not your fault, and the lack of manners is hers. You can say, 'No; it's not that kind of evening,' (this sentence doesn't need to mean anything particular), or 'I've planned the numbers carefully,' or just 'I can't fit anyone else round the table,' (this one had better show some signs of being true), but you could also say, 'I can only entertain a very limited number because I don't have enough plates/cutlery/glasses, etc.' Watch out for the thick-skinned who offer to lend you more plates!

You might well not mind at all having extras: if your entertaining style is casual and your resources ample, then by all means express enthusiasm for the new guest. You may, however, draw the line at guests of a different generation from the rest of your friends. It is perfectly reasonable to enquire about the extra person and then say, 'I'm not sure if it's going to be your mother's/twelve-year-old niece's kind of thing – she won't know anyone after all.' In the end, remember it's up to you whom you invite.

If Guests Bring Something

Of course their wine or sweets may be inferior to yours, but, in general, try to look grateful and use whatever it is. If they bring sweet German wine, then that's probably what they like and they'll drink it even if everyone else prefers your vintage burgundy. When offering a first drink you could say, 'Perhaps you'd like some of your own wine?' They may look enthusiastic (in which case open it immediately) or neutral (open theirs unless you had something already planned) or positively shifty (it was either the cheapest in the shop or left over from their last party – put their bottle aside for cooking or, of course, the next bottle party).

6

ATTENDING DINNER PARTIES

When you're invited – well, you know what to do first, don't you? Thank your hostess for the kind invitation. Usually these days it will have been issued in person or over the phone so you're replying straightaway. Sound enthusiastic. Answer the invitation as quickly as possible, as firmly as possible.

Stalling Invitations

If you're really not sure if you can come, then tell your hostess and take your lead from her. Say, 'My mother is going into hospital some time this month, and it could be then. I'd hate to let you down if that happened, but obviously I'd have to go, so shall I just say "No" now?' This gives your hostess a chance to say, 'No, of course not. We'll plan for your coming but if you have to cancel, then, of course, I'll understand,' or not, as she chooses. This sample excuse is the kind of thing no-one will mind of course, and most hostesses will say, 'Come if you can,' and not cancel the invitation.

Usually people's reasons for not committing themselves are less praiseworthy, and they often make it embarrassingly clear that they would like to come to dinner if nothing better comes up in the meantime. (I suppose this is preferable to people who accept and then dump at the last minute if something better does come up.) It is neither polite nor tactful to say, 'I'd like to come but I know someone else is planning to invite me out some time in that week for a really super theatre evening and I wouldn't like it to clash . . .' Either think of another excuse or refuse or accept *and stick to it* – it's the other evening that will have to be re-arranged. The first accepted invitation gets priority.

Bringing Friends

Don't say: 'Can I bring my boyfriend?' or 'My old schoolfriend/ mother is staying with me right then, may I bring her along?'

Do say: 'Is it a couples type of thing? Are people bringing partners or do you want just me?' or 'I don't think I'll be able to come that night because I have an old friend staying.'

These responses give your hostess the chance to be gracious and say, 'By all means bring him along,' or else to indicate gently that she has all the guests she needs. If it's your mother staying, you'd better make sure your hostess isn't obliged to have you both. It has to be said that parents and other relatives can be very nice and very good company, and yours may be exceptionally broad-minded and right-thinking, but it's rather unfair to impose them on someone else's dinner party. It just is. Same as people who want to bring their children. If you think your mother is good company, invite people round to your house (or a restaurant) to meet her, then next time she comes your friends may feel they know her well enough to ask her out. (Many people would have good reason for not wanting their mother to be present at a rather unzipped social event – your friends may well reveal things about you that you'd rather she didn't know.)

If you're vegetarian, then first read the section on veggie guests (page 52).

You must tell your hostess as soon as she invites you. You have an absolute obligation to do this, and it is *very* bad manners not to. If you receive an invitation via a third party ('Jane invited us both to eat with her after the film, so I said we would'), then you must check that your friend told Jane and, if she didn't, then you must ring Jane yourself.

No matter how aggressive a vegetarian you are, you are still the one who is different, so you must take steps. It is no use saying, 'But she knows perfectly well I'm vegetarian.' Why should she? It is a form of arrogance to assume that other people's interest in you is so all-embracing. Unless you eat there once a week, you must say, 'You do know' (or 'remember' if you must) 'that I don't eat meat, don't you?' People don't remember these things necessarily, any more than they remember if you drink red or white wine or don't like chocolate.

Other Food Preferences

If you have some other special preference or allergy – well, if you've had it for some time you probably know what the percentage is in telling the hostess beforehand. If you are on some new diet or have a recent medical problem, then it's as well to say. But, in all honesty, you should offer to withdraw if your problems are particularly difficult, or offer to come for the chat and the company but not to eat.

Roughly speaking, if there's a major food group you can't eat, then you should say. (Even if you personally will be quite willing to eat potato and vegetables, it will embarrass your cook. Also the cook may be planning an all-in-one dish which means you don't have the option.) If it's an ingredient which you can fish out, or eat a little of, or don't mind if it's sufficiently mashed up, then say nothing.

But if you haven't told the hostess beforehand, then you can't tell her at all, unless the situation is life-threatening. If you have a deadly allergy, then you must say, just in case, no matter how unusual or unlikely the ingredient is. What you must not do is say, just as the plate is put in front of you, 'There isn't any garlic in this, is there? Because I can't eat garlic.'

If you are going to do that, then you had better own up to it being a deadly allergy *straightaway* because otherwise there is a terrible temptation for the cook to say, 'What? Garlic? In this? Of course not,' no matter what the truth. (If you are a very bad guest, then the 'deadly' bit might make it even more tempting for the cook to say that there's no garlic in it.)

It is not good manners to say, 'Oh, if you could just rustle me up an omelette or something, that's fine.' Lots of people don't like making omelettes for other people, and hardly anyone wants to make an omelette while they are finishing off and serving up a completely different three-dish meal for seven others.

And, before you suggest it, even less do they want you in the kitchen making the omelette. 'Bread and cheese' is a better suggestion if you really feel you must ask for something.

At the Dinner Party
Well, after all that worrying about the invitation and the food preferences you are finally about to go to the party.

First, read the earlier section on basic table manners. Your meals with friends may be more informal so not all the rules apply, but it does no harm to know what the rules are.

What to take: the obvious choices are wine, flowers, choco-lates. Another possibility might be some high quality or exotic fruit or biscuits. The idea is that you give something consumable or perishable, not a permanent object. If you drink a lot, then wine is a good idea (makes you popular and decreases the chances of the booze running out) but most people are grateful for the other choices too. In general, bring something *you* like: it's not selfish to follow your own tastes rather than trying to predict the likes of a table-full.

Getting to Drink Your Own Wine

One problem that bothers a lot of people is this: bringing something to a dinner party and not being invited to consume it. It may be that you are quite happy for your wine to go into the rack while something better, carefully matched to the meal, is produced, but most people are convinced that the opposite is what happens. If you brought the last of your carefully chosen and imported wines from your French holiday, and all you get offered is supermarket plonk, then you have cause for complaint.

I think this is often just a lack of communication or a result of the host's general fluster, and a little action on the part of the guest can take care of most situations. First of all, you should stress as you hand it over, 'We've been saving this for a special occasion/We chose this one specially for this evening.' If you have brought white wine or champagne, then you can say, 'I've been chilling it, but can you put it in your fridge so we can drink it soon?'

Such remarks are reasonable and, in fact, helpful. Your host/ess may genuinely forget, or not be sure which bottle to open next, or may have chosen wines to go specially with the meal. Whatever people might tell you, most people can't tell whether a bottle is good or not after a quick look at it so they may be grateful for hints. I'm all for people being honest: 'I brought this, it's cheap but good for sloshing down,' (especially if you're a noted slosher-down yourself) or 'This, I hope, is quite nice, we got it in France . . .'

If your host asks what you want to drink, then there's no reason not to say, 'Well, I'd quite like some of my wine,' possibly in a self-deprecating tone and possibly adding, 'If you were going to open it anyway.' If you want an extra push on opening yours, then you can invent (or even know) some reason why it's interesting or why you want to taste it. This is another ploy to be pushed when you hand it over: 'This is on special offer/My off-licence recommends it/Read about it in a mag – and I'm dying to taste it/Need to know whether to go ahead and buy a case/Really would like your opinion on it.' Fairly unmistakable hints.

If your host doesn't pick up on any of these, then there's not much else you can do. If you go somewhere regularly and are fed up with your wine being swallowed into their racks, then you can try one last ploy: bring a red wine, *already opened*, and say, 'This needs two hours to breathe so it's just about ready to drink now.' You'd better have a wine that looks worth the bother for this (i.e. not supermarket plonk or Beaujolais nouveau) or at least looks obscure. But this is last-ditch stuff, for use if your anxiety is to get drinkable wine rather than make friends or behave normally. The other option with people you visit regularly is to bring cheap wine so you don't care.

Flowers: you can't necessarily expect the cook to stop imme-diately and make a lovely arrangement, but you could ask for a jam-jar to shove them in if you think they're going to die from lying waterless in their paper on top of the piano.

Chocolates: these are easily forgotten. If you are on friendly relations with the hostess, then at coffee-time you can say, 'I know what would go really well with this,' or some such. If cook has had a bad evening, then I hope she's hard-faced enough to say, 'And I'll enjoy them very much with my coffee tomorrow, thank you very much.' If some other (even if very inferior) chocs are produced, then you've probably had it; you've got no hope of seeing yours again. (Except possibly at the next dinner party or the next party your hostess goes to. Boxes of chocs can be as bad as cheap wine for doing the rounds as the brought item.)

I once offered someone a mint after dinner. He looked at the box for a moment and then said, 'I don't want one of those but I did notice that up on that shelf you have a box of delicious continental chocs, and I'd like one of them.' I promised I'd put him in my book as a Bad Example, and here he is.

What to do if:

Someone is Rude to You:
You have to work out for yourself the skein of obligations to your host. Consider how rude the guest meant to be – he may simply be unthinking or not know something relevant about you. Was he drunk? A trip out to another room may be needed

to calm down/think it over. If you want to walk out, a 'headache' – not meant to fool anyone – is dignified and polite. You should explain to your hostess in case she's completely unaware of what's going on. (If it is the hostess who's been rude, then you have fewer options.)

If someone is very rude to you and you are upset, then in my view you have every right to remove yourself from the situation. You don't have the right to demand someone else's removal, in fact you very rarely do unless you are in your own room/house/office, but you always have the right to remove yourself. However, I should warn you of something: very oddly, sympathy can veer away from someone who leaves the party, and the gossipers left behind can work something up about you. This is wrong and ludicrous, but experience shows it's true. Haven't you ever been in a group that watched one member stomp off? Did you hear much good said of him afterwards? You don't have to stay and fight if you don't want to, but when you phone a fellow guest the next day don't assume she'll be full of sympathy and saying, 'We gave that Pat a hard time after you went, I can tell you – I'd have left myself in sympathy with you but I had to stay and speak my mind about what he said to you.' She's more likely to say, 'Everyone thought it was a bit odd your leaving that way – what was the matter?' Sad but true.

You Break/Spill Something

You should offer profuse apologies and regrets. Try to clear up or help, but stop if it's obvious the hostess would prefer to clear up herself. Ask what you can do to make amends. Make it obvious you are sorry, regretful, but don't go on about it, do let the party continue. If it was a real calamity, then at the end of the evening get the hostess alone and offer to pay, replace, dry-clean. Don't make a nuisance of yourself, but don't take 'No' for an answer unless it's very convincingly said, along with some magic words like, 'It's covered by the insurance and I always hated it, so please don't worry.' Apologize again and offer more reparations the next day or the next time you see them. Don't offer to pay, meaning it, and then expect them to ask you for the money once they know how much is involved – they will be waiting for you to offer again and are unlikely to show you the bill without being pressed.

Unless huge sums of money are involved or there is a huge disparity in your incomes, most people won't actually expect you to pay and will try not to mind too much. But that is dependent on your accepting the blame and apologizing. What is despicable and makes people very angry is to attempt to get out of it, to blame someone else, to be cautious about accepting that we did it. Unfortunately, we are all ordered to behave like this by motor insurers, who say we must never say sorry after a car accident. This is sadly creeping into other areas of life and is both unpleasant and counter-productive. If you need a selfish argument: if you say sorry and apologize, your victim is a lot more likely to say, 'Don't worry, it was rather near the edge and very fragile, I don't want you to replace it.' If you try to wriggle out and say, 'I didn't touch it, you put it in a stupid place,' they are likely to get mad and want to get even.

It is possible to extend one's own household insurance to cover dreadful things you do in someone else's house. This would be worth it if you do such things all the time, but if you're that kind of person you're unlikely to get round to organizing insurance, making claims, etc.

Smoking

These days I would say that you can't smoke unless your host lights up first. Otherwise, if you must have a cigarette, you go outside.

Thank Yous

It's usually enough to thank your host when you leave and perhaps thank them again next time you see them – 'I really enjoyed your party the other night, thank you very much.' Phoning the next day to say the same thing is very polite. Some people do write their thanks, perhaps on a greetings card, and this is ultra-polite, but not essential. Of course, if you had a particularly good time or the party was in your honour or it was some special occasion, then it is a good idea to write a line of thanks. This needn't be long, and sending a postcard or blank greetings card is a good idea: 'Thank you so much for a lovely evening – I enjoyed every minute of it. You must have gone to a lot of trouble, but believe me it was worth it, and everyone appreciated it.'

7

GIVING AND ATTENDING INFORMAL PARTIES

Invitations

The really important information that guests need and hosts should do their best to provide is 'Exactly how informal?' Party-givers complain all the time that guests behave badly: they arrive late/early, they bring extra people, they don't bring a bottle, they eat all the food/ate before they came. Of course, that's hard on hosts, but it could be just the result of misunderstandings.

These are the questions a guest wants answers to:

'How dressed up will it be?'

'May I bring a friend?'

'Will there be food, and will it be snacks or something more substantial (i.e. should I eat beforehand)?'

'Should I bring a bottle?'

'Is it a celebration, e.g. a birthday, requiring me to bring a present?'

'What time should I come? If I can't make it at that time, is it OK to come much later or not?'

'What time will it be over?'

If you are a guest, then you are at liberty to ask these questions, as tactfully as possible – 'Is it a drinks and nibbles party?' is easier to answer than, 'Are you providing my evening meal?'

Hosts should try to provide as much of this information as they can in their invitations (whether written or oral). If you're young and poor, then say, 'Please bring a bottle,' or 'It's a bottle party.' Say 'It'll be very informal – do bring someone if you'd like to.' This does actually imply that they can bring one person but not twenty. If it's someone you don't know very well (a colleague, say), you could add, if appropriate, 'But no need to – there'll be plenty of people there you know.'

Most hosts will be happy to accommodate visiting friends at a party: but do ask. An open-ended question, 'I've actually got a couple of old school friends staying that weekend . . .???' on a rising note will probably produce an, 'Oh, by all means bring them along,' response.

In fact, hosts are right to welcome such extra guests, as new blood is definitely a good thing (although, if you bring total strangers to a party, then it is your job to look after them to some extent, make sure they're meeting people and not standing there like lost souls).

Bottles

As people get older and richer, they tend to expect to provide more of the alcohol at a party they are hosting, but it's fair to say that it's never wrong or bad manners to arrive with a bottle. But you don't have to. It's a generous gesture but, if you don't drink much, then don't feel obliged to buy expensive wine every time you go somewhere. If you drink a lot, you should scale up your contribution accordingly, and if you are a couple who expect to be drinking solidly from 9 pm to 4 am then, if you ask me, it's a bit mean to bring one bottle between you. Hosts: don't forget to supply lots of soft drinks and mixers.

Gatecrashers

If you're worried about gatecrashers, then think beforehand which are your strongest and most reliable friends who can help you deal with the situation. Take action immediately if you have reason to be suspicious of anyone. If a number of people are giving a party, then it can be difficult, but it's very reasonable to say politely, 'Do tell me whose guest you are?'

If you live on a main road in a big town, you may even get people just passing and trying it on. I don't say this lightly but:

Fig. 7. Don't forget to provide lots of soft drinks and mixers.

call the police if things look touchy. Tell them you're calling the police. If nothing else, say in a loud voice, 'OK Pete, can you call the police NOW.' There are two reasons I say this: (1) Violence can get out of hand in far less time than you think, and in far more respectable situations than you think. And it *definitely* isn't worth it, even if it makes you look uncool or breaks up the party, to have any kind of heavy friction going on. It could turn into fighting: stop it before it starts. (2) However piratical and exciting they sound, gatecrashers are strangers. Do you want total strangers wandering round your house with no supervision at all? They could be criminals. They could steal from you or your guests, they could be drug dealers. A friend may go home with one of them, thinking him another friend of yours.

Keeping Guests Happy
Hosts often leave large informal parties to run themselves. They are, of course, entitled to do this, and it may be what their friends expect, but if you want to be more than just the supplier of rooms, these are the main points to watch:

1. Keep moving round the different areas, so you know what's going on and who's there. Try not to stay in one spot for a long time, talking to one group of people. Guests should circulate, but so should hosts. Don't join up with your two best friends and stay in one corner making

private jokes, getting drunk and eyeing up members of the
opposite sex, even if this is what the three of you do at
everyone else's parties.

2. Keep an eye out for people whom you don't know (ask
    politely who they are, and take action accordingly – see
    above) or people obviously on their own or dying to talk to
    someone or to meet someone. As the host, it is very easy
    for you to introduce people and you should do so as much
    as possible. If you have trustworthy close friends you can
    get them to do the same or you can merely press-gang
    them into talking to the lonely bore in the corner.

3. Look out for anyone who is very unhappy or very drunk
    or being given a hard time by other guests. *Interfere* in all
    these cases. Unhappy guests should be offered help. Drunk
    guests should be watched carefully and sent home or
    allowed to lie down or given into the hands of their own
    friends (depending on how aggressive and unpleasant they
    are). If you see a guest being bullied or harassed, then you
    should ask that guest – ignoring the harasser – 'Are you
    OK?' or 'Everything all right here?' or 'Is there anything
    you can't handle here?' and listen for the tone of voice as
    much as the reply.

Many people feel they can't make a scene at a friend's party and
put up with behaviour they wouldn't stand for a second anywhere else. Good hosts ensure they don't have to. If you have
male friends who don't know how to behave around females,
then you have a duty to watch out that they are not making your
female guests unhappy. Or better still, don't invite them: 'He gets
like that when he's drunk,' is no excuse.

Ending the Party
When you want the party to end then your, admittedly hard,
task will be made much easier if you are quite sure in your own
mind that it is perfectly reasonable to send everyone home now.
The major factor keeping the party going could easily be your
own lurking doubts about being a spoilsport or a wet blanket, a
worry that you're being terribly uncool or rude in ending the
event. But if you make one or two polite indications that the
party is over and they are ignored, then there is nothing rude

about getting more forceful in asking people to go. Some people recommend flashing the lights on and off to end the party. It is an unfortunate but realistic fact about life today that the key action may well be to cut off the supply of drink. Hide it, lock it up, say it's all gone. Whatever. Then you can offer coffee first (though this means people who might otherwise have been ready to leave sit round saying, 'I love this time at a party, don't you?') and then coats and taxis with increasing frequency and force.

Guests

Security

Parties are very open affairs. Don't take valuables with you, leave everything but your taxi fare at home. Women at large informal events should keep their bags with them (or better still don't bring one or wear a little purse bag on a long strap across your chest). It's plain foolish to leave them in a bedroom or the kitchen. And don't be too sure of anyone you meet there. Unless he obviously knows the same people you do, then you should treat him as warily as someone you met on the top of the bus: i.e. be friendly if you like the look of him and he seems trustworthy, but don't take any risks and obey a few simple security rules. A party, even if it's hosted by your best friend, is a large public event full of strangers.

Meeting People

The old clichéd situations are best. Hang around the food and drink tables, and fall into conversation about the cheese if you have to. Everyone makes vague general remarks at food tables, 'Gosh, he must have gone to a lot of trouble/Could I have the knife after you?/Have you any idea what this is?' so you won't be instantly labelled as lonely and on the pick-up. Kitchens are the classic place for talking and (despite the old pop song) some of the best people hang around there. Be brave: listen carefully to one or two conversations (while spending a long time choosing your drink or finding the corkscrew), find one you like the sound of, or feel you could contribute to, and break into it. That's what people do at parties, it's not at all odd. You think all those little groups of people are all great friends discussing mutual interests, but the chances are most of them scarcely know each other. Once in a blue moon you may get the immediate impression you've blundered: the group looks at you curiously, you feel unwelcome, no-one answers you. This is, I must admit, fairly shattering. You just have to move away immediately, saying, 'Oh, need more tonic in this,' and keep telling yourself the truth: this is very unusual. Try again; I promise you most times it won't be like that.

There is one small warning: try not to sound too aggressive when you break in, unless that's very much your personal style and you're happy with it. If people are discussing private education in a generally sympathetic way, and you're anti, then either phrase it tactfully (at least to begin with) or find a different conversation.

Guests in a conversational circle should always try to be welcoming to outsiders – it's good to try to make a small effort on this. New blood often helps the conversation along anyway.

If the party has dancing, then in this day and age anyone can ask anyone else to dance. Dancing in groups with (shock! horror!) uneven numbers is almost universal at parties. If you want to dance, it doesn't matter who with. If you want to meet someone, then ask him. Be prepared to take no for an answer though: some people hate dancing, nothing personal, nothing to do with you, and shouldn't be dragged onto the floor. You must be able to take a refusal graciously, even if it is your favourite record.

One more thing about meeting people/making friends at parties when you're looking for a romance: the worst possible thing to do is to ignore everyone who has no potential (wrong sex, not up to your high standards). If you'll talk to anyone, if you make friends easily, then you have more to talk about, you're more attractive, you do more, you get invited to more events – and then you will meet people you fancy.

8

STAYING THE NIGHT WITH GOOD FRIENDS

If you're going back with a friend after a good night out and you're going to doss down on his floor or share her bed, then you know each other well enough to have worked out your own rules and etiquette.

If it's more of a proper visit than that, then you should keep the following rules:

Bring What You Need with You
I'm assuming clean clothes are taken for granted.

1. Nightwear. Even if you don't always wear it at home, your friend might prefer it for various reasons. It's essential if you don't know the exact set-up where you're going – who knows what you might see on your way to the loo?

2. Towel. Many hostesses will provide this, but best not to presume on a first visit – young poor hosts may not have extra clean towels to go round. If you forget, then do explain and ask for one. If one is provided anyway, you'll know for next time.

3. Washbag. The minimum is probably your toothbrush. Some people bring their own toothpaste and soap – this seems extra polite but I think most hosts would assume they would provide this for you. If you go through elaborate face-cleansing rituals you'll need to bring your own stuff. You yourself know whether (this applies particularly

to women) you'd feel happy to assume you can borrow the hostess's cleansers, deodorant, make-up or perfume. Most women entertaining other women say, 'Do help yourself to anything you see in the bathroom and ask if there's anything you need.' Women guests also like trying out something new: even if they've brought their own shampoo they'll ask if they can try the hostess's, for interest. All this to some extent depends on your travelling circumstances: if you're arriving by car you can bring a whole beauty-box full; public transport may limit your carrying capacity.

Make it Clear Exactly When You Expect to Arrive and Depart

Sometimes one hesitates to say, 'I'll arrive in time for dinner,' (if not going specifically for dinner) as it sounds as though you're demanding food. But, of course, the one thing all hostesses want is to know how many meals you're down for. So you say: 'I guess it would be about 8ish – is that all right?'

'Fine – so you'll be wanting supper then?'

'Well, if that's all right – but I could eat on the way.'

'No, no. I'll do supper – unless that's too late for you?'

'Well, I could eat before I leave . . .'

'No, no. I'll do something.'

In this conversation both sides very much would like dinner at the host house on arrival, but you'd never know. They're both trying to be polite and not impose their desires on the other side. In general, a host expecting an overnight guest probably is going to be geared up to producing a meal on arrival, so if it's offered be happy to accept.

You should ring if you're going to be much later than you said, even if you were fairly vague. People do wait in for guests, and if they knew you weren't coming until later it might be quite helpful. If you're going to be much earlier, it's not quite so important, but . . . no matter how casual you and your friend are, he or she may be counting on all that time for getting ready.

You may arrive to find host in the bath, bed not made, supper still in tins. 'I don't mind all that, not a bit,' you shout gaily, but the point is that your host may mind very much. If you can, then do warn him.

Bring Something with You

Some small present – a food or drink contribution is, yet again, one of the best ideas. A bottle of wine or a box of chocolates is fine, or else a bunch of flowers. You may feel you are making too much of a normal overnight stay, but hardly any hosts would feel that way, especially if you bring something you are going to share anyway. People have you to stay for love, but overnight guests are a trouble and an inconvenience and you should try to minimize the trouble. If you're very poor, or you stay over every week and it's treated by everyone very matter-of-factly, then it's still nice to take a packet of biscuits or a bar of chocolate from time to time.

Sleeping Arrangements

If you're travelling by car, and it suits your and your friend's style, then offer to bring a duvet or sleeping-bag. No-one will mind the offer, even if they've got capacity to sleep a football team.

Other Residents

Most flatmates are cheerfully welcoming or vague and unnoticing, but your presence will make a difference to their lives, and you should try to minimize that. If two people share a flat – and a bathroom – then the presence of just one extra person can make a big difference, especially if you're all trying to get up and out at the same time next morning. You shouldn't need telling this, but you are not there on equal terms with the residents: you don't really get a vote on what's watched on the TV; try not to get in their way in the kitchen; if you're hoping for a long bath, then check that's OK with all residents.

The Next Morning

If your arrangements were obviously temporary (i.e. sofa bed in the living-room), then this is easy. You remove the bedding, re-assemble the sofa, and pile the bedding neatly on top of it or behind it. Even if you are staying more than one night on the sofa bed, then you should still do this every morning – anything

else is very unfair on the permanent residents. (If your friend
shares a flat and you're sleeping in the living-room, then to be
super-polite you should match your getting-up time to the
earliest riser in the flat, unless you are given cast-iron assurances
that it's all right.) After your last night you take the pillows from
their cases, separate sheets from blankets or duvet from duvet
cover, and leave linen to be washed in a separate pile from the
blankets, pillows, etc.

If you're sleeping in the spare room, then it's slightly more
difficult. You could strip the bed completely when your stay is
over, though many people merely turn the covers back. If you
have stayed only one night, there is always the unspoken feeling
that it's almost a waste to wash all those sheets when they've
scarcely been touched. The other unspoken fear is: *perhaps they
don't want me to see the mattress.* These are not really matters
you can discuss with the hostess. If you ask her what she wants
you to do, she'll almost certainly say, 'Oh, just leave it, I'll do it.'
(A prize for the hostess who says, 'Actually, I'd quite like you to
take the sheets to the launderette before you go!') Asking the
hostess is probably best if you're really tormented by the problem, but I think it makes you feel better without your actually
helping at all; you know in your heart she'll say, 'Don't bother,'
but you think she'll consider you polite for asking – and this is
not good etiquette at all.

Afterwards
Thank them, thank them, thank them. Well, you knew what was
coming, didn't you? This is the watershed point: if people have
had you to stay, then you send them a written thank you.
Exceptions are: (a) if you paid them; (b) if you're lovers; (c)
staying with immediate family if you look on that as going home
rather than staying; or (d) (just about) if you stay somewhere
regularly on a semi-formal basis; or (e) (just about) if you slept
on the floor after a party.

The thank you doesn't have to be formal and it can be quite
short if that's all you can manage. (Better a short note on a
postcard than nothing at all.) If you just stayed the night, then
a postcard is fine. If you spent some time there or had elaborate
meals or entertainment laid on, then you really ought to try to
write something appreciative (though, yet again, better a short
scribble than nothing – if you keep leaving the letter 'until I've
got time to do it properly', then write something short NOW).

If you know you won't write (and it is a terrible failure), then phone when you get home. You can say, 'I just thought I'd let you know I got back safely, and I'd like to thank you for being so kind to me.' If you stay with people before going to the airport, then you have the ideal opportunity to send them a thank you postcard from your exotic destination.

9

MORE ON VISITS AND STAYING OVER

Staying with People of an Older Generation
This is generally going to mean parents – your own or someone else's – but includes everyone you suspect has more formal standards than your own.

It's not very different from staying with your friends (assuming you treat your friends as politely as you should) but you may have to be more on the alert. Make a conscious effort to be extra-polite, and you should get through.

If you stay with a friend at his parents' house, then he will help. But one word of warning: in his attempts to be friendly and polite to you, and to make you feel relaxed, he may say about all kinds of things, 'Oh yes, that'll be fine, my Mum won't mind at all.' Both of you might be surprised.

I'm having to take a rather stereotyped view of the young and old sectors in this visit, picturing you (the visitor) as some young, bohemian, thoughtless flat-sharer, untidy and casual, and your hosts as a sedate, middle-aged, middle-class couple who are very tidy and house-proud. Of course, you're not all like that, but after viewing the hardest scenario, then you'll find it much easier when your older hosts turn out to be ageing hippies with a relaxed view of life, or if you are really a young fogey with strict and perfect manners.

All the guidelines for staying with friends apply: bring what you need with you, bring a small present (chocs or flowers may be safest – older people may not drink wine, or, alternatively, may like much better vintages than you can afford, or may worry about why you feel the need to bring your own wine), be polite and considerate round the house, and thank them afterwards. If staying with a couple, it is normal to offer your most heartfelt thanks, and the present, to the female, on the grounds that it is she who has done most of the work of having you.

Other points that might arise:

1. Offer to help. This is polite and correct. Your host may not want you to do a thing, but offer at least twice. It's always better to offer to do something specific (it shows willing): 'Let me help you with those dishes,' or 'Perhaps I can set the table?' Don't push it too much if you're told not to help. Many people don't want strangers in their kitchen and may be embarrassed if you rush to clear the table and carry everything through.

2. Be very tidy in any public rooms: don't leave your stuff lying around. Your older friends may well have higher standards than you, and it's unfair on them: they may mind very much if their own friends come round and you've made the living-room look like your own room in your own flat. The same applies to the bathroom (true when visiting anywhere but particularly with older friends). Keep your things in a washbag, fold (or remove) your towels, wipe down the bath, mop up overflow from the floor. Every time.

    It is best to assume that you cannot smoke in the house – go outside if you have to.

3. When you visit your friend, you may expect to treat his place like your own. This does not apply to your friend's parents. Don't invite people round or use the phone without asking permission (and paying, particularly if it's long-distance), or leave the phone number with all and sundry.

    Don't assume you can use the TV or stereo, and don't help yourself to food from the kitchen, unless you have been specifically told you may do those things.

4. Try to be friendly. Don't think that you have no sociable obligations to your older hosts. Make a point of chatting to them – over mealtimes for example. Don't sit silently,

relying on your friend to talk to his parents and speaking only to him. Try at least once over the visit to talk to your hosts alone. Ask them to show you their garden or get into a discussion of a TV programme they like.

5. Try to be tactful about your friend. Stories about how he got drunk on his birthday are probably not a good idea. It's surprising how many people don't think before speaking about this – they forget that what is endearing and charming to them may be horrifying to parents. Watch out for some sudden silence in conversation when you've said something: you may have (all unawares) revealed something the parents didn't know. Often this is something you couldn't have predicted or planned for, and you don't even know why it's a problem. (Your friend is joining a new religion, is quitting his job, has a new girlfriend.) Perhaps your friend was just waiting for the right moment to tell them, but you've just jumped in with both feet. Pretend you haven't noticed that anything is wrong and move the conversation along as quickly and smoothly as you can to another subject. They'll have to sort it out among themselves, but the less you say, the more leeway it gives your mate to make up the ground: he can say you were mistaken, that he hasn't really decided at all – you overstated the case, it's only *just* happened.

Staying with Your Own Parents After You've Left Home

The difference between this and other visits is that you become a member of the household much more than in other places. Parents (you hope) don't expect to entertain you every second. You are left to your own devices, probably have a front door key and your own room again, come and go more or less as you please. You might say, 'I won't be in for supper tonight,' which would (probably) be very bad etiquette when visiting someone else, but is accepted by your mother with, 'Fine, have a nice time.'

Families vary: ideally when you grow up and leave home, on your return both sides agree that you are now adults, but favoured adults with special privileges and duties. If parents and children *want* to regress when the children come home, then etiquette has nothing to do with it. The hints for both sides that follow are offered as help for those who are looking for a better way.

Offspring
Should try not to complain that things have been changed. If you don't live there any more, then you shouldn't be surprised if the decor is different, your favourite chair has been thrown out or re-covered, or there aren't bacon sandwiches for Saturday breakfast. You should also be prepared for your old room to be used for other purposes, and should be ready to remove all possessions from your old rooms if asked.

On a visit don't pretend you live there still and treat it like home (which, as we all know, means treating it as a hotel). Don't assume you can use the phone without permission or eat anything you find or invite people round or that your mother will do your washing. You may be convinced that you can do all these things, but it is not polite. Children say, 'But my mother *likes* doing my washing,' and this may be true of some mothers. However, for every hundred children who say this, it is hard to find even one mother who will say as much as, 'Well, he brought all his washing home, I suppose I don't really mind doing it.'

You can gratefully accept when they offer help ranging from old furniture to cash handouts, to food to take back to your flat. You should not take this for granted, but thank them properly. You should always remember their birthdays, Mother's Day (if they like that sort of thing) and Christmas with presents which are thoughtful if not expensive. Poverty is never an excuse for not giving presents.

You should try to ensure that a visit to your parents is not a drain on their resources. Be very careful about things like the phone bill and the heating. You may be surprised by what economies they now practise, especially if they have retired, and what a difference it can make if a thoughtless visitor won't conform. Your parents may be reluctant to explain these things to you, from pride or fear or appearing to be begging. Parents can foolishly think their children need money more than they do, and can be very reluctant to ask for help.

Don't think you will ever be rich enough not to need gifts of food made or grown by your parents. Never refuse such items.

Parents
Should work hard at remembering that their children are not
teenagers any more. They should be allowed to go out and do
what they like. They should not be subjected to embarrassing
reminiscences, nor should they be shown off to friends and
relatives like a prize dog. Don't make too many elaborate plans
for your offspring without checking first. They may have been
looking forward to a quiet rest, or (particularly if you still live in
the place they grew up in) may hope to see their own old friends.

Don't be surprised if producing a favourite old aunt or a
favourite old recipe brings forth the revelation that the offspring
never liked either of them, ever, but never dared say so before.
Don't be too sure that you know what your children think about
things. Parents sometimes have a penchant for re-writing history,
particularly as regards childhood. If you want to try reminiscences ('Remember how we all looked forward all year to our
summer holiday?'), then be prepared for some possibly harsh
home truths. Parents, for some reason, think that their memories
are more accurate, but the truth is that children have nothing
else to remember for that period, and independent checking
between siblings bears out the idea that children remember their
own childhood best.

Despite all this, it is up to parents to set ground rules for a
visit. You may think that your children behave thoughtlessly and
inconsiderately, but it may simply never have crossed their minds
that this is the case. Children do tend to believe firmly that you
like them to act as if they were at home. If you brought them up
properly, then you should be able to ask them to help (if they
haven't offered) by going to the shops or laying the table, and
you should also have sufficient clout to ask them not to use the
phone without contributing to the bill, nor to pinch the newspaper for the whole morning, nor the entire week's supply of
biscuits. Children are *quite* likely to say, 'Oh, it didn't occur to
me that that's what I was doing and that you'd mind, I'm terribly
sorry,' and they might even try to reform.

Bringing Your Partner Home
This is the classic problem. You're staying at your parents with
your long-standing romantic partner. You sleep together in your
own home – why not at your parents'? This is more a matter for
family custom than etiquette, but there is one point to be made.
The simple fact is that you can ask to share a bedroom with

someone, but you cannot insist. A tactful way to put it might be, 'You can put us both in together if you like – that might make life easier for you.'

But if your parents, in their own house, do not want you to sleep in the same bed as your boyfriend, then that is their absolute right. You may think it hypocritical or stupid or impractical, but it is not your house and you do not have the right to insist on anything else. It is arrogant to think that your own principles take precedence. If you were eating at the home of a vegetarian, would you insist that they cooked meat just for you?

Perhaps you and your family just like a good ding-dong on this kind of subject and enjoy parading how different your standards are. That's fine. But it is ridiculous to pretend that a couple are going to be greatly put out by spending one night apart: if you were travelling on a night train with single berths, would you be so upset?

I should stress that this is just an etiquette point. If you feel that your parents refuse to accept you as an adult, that it is their way of saying they disapprove of your partner, then that is a family problem and nothing to do with manners. But on an etiquette level you have no right to make that sort of demand on any hosts, including your parents.

Visits in General – Sleeping Arrangements

Wherever you are visiting, you accept whatever is provided. The only exception is if you are travelling with someone that your host may wrongly think is a romantic partner. It's important to sort this out beforehand. It is very embarrassing saying, 'He's not my boyfriend, just a friend, we don't sleep together, we'll need separate beds,' particularly if your future host says, 'Well, of course not, didn't assume so for a moment, naturally separate beds,' with a note of umbrage in his voice – but it's not nearly as embarrassing as getting there and finding a huge double bed ready for you. If faced with this, take your host quietly aside and ask if you can sleep on the sofa. You have to ask for, and accept, minimum standards in replacement accommodation, but you do not have to share a bed with someone if you'd rather not.

If you are having people to stay and you're not sure, you say to them, 'How many bedrooms [or 'beds' if the second person will have to sleep on the sofa] will you need?' This is a perfectly reasonable non-judgmental question which anyone should be able to answer without the slightest embarrassment. If you really can't bring yourself to ask it, then you'd better be prepared (in your mind) for either possibility when they arrive, with blankets ready to put on the sofa. If you have two beds in one room: same sex guests can be asked to share. Opposite sex guests may well be willing, but you ought to check discreetly with them separately or with the one you know better or with the woman – whoever seems most likely to object or to give an accurate answer.

Same sex guests in one bed: again, something some people think nothing of and other people find very off-putting. Only offer it as an alternative. Say, 'You can either sleep together in the double bed or one gets the double and the other has a mattress on the floor.' Whoever objects to the first arrangement has, of course, to take the mattress option.

Points for the Good Host or Hostess

You should try to keep your guests as well-informed as possible. Make sure they know where everything is, particularly the light switches. When you have guests it is polite to leave passage lights on as much as possible and certainly while you are all up and awake: I know you're trying to save electricity and the world, but it is awful trying to find your way around a strange, dark house. I'm astonished by people who, when entertaining dinner or overnight guests, go to endless trouble to prepare the appropriate rooms and the bathroom, but give not the slightest thought as to how their guests are going to get from one to the other, because they themselves know where all the light switches are and can switch on and – regrettably – off as they go.

With overnight guests, you should also explain if there are any double-locking arrangements for the front door, so they can get out if there's a fire or even go and get your early morning croissants next day. You should give them some idea of who else is in the house: you may feel they don't need to know about your lodger or midnight lover, but they may well meet him in the kitchen or outside the bathroom so it's only fair to warn them. (It's particularly important for female guests who may wander round half-clad on the assumption that there are no strangers about.) If they are sleeping on the sofa in the living-room, it's important that they know that the dark figure lumbering in and passing through is merely a flatmate. And, of course, you must keep your flatmates up to date so they're not too surprised to find a stranger on the sofa, and aren't expecting to claim it for their own friend.

Try to think ahead what guests may need: give them an idea of what the timings are for the morning and invite them to use the kitchen if they get up earlier. Remember to provide towels for them. Leave out an extra blanket (or tell them where to find one) no matter how warm you think it is: it's somehow always colder for overnight guests, and there's nothing worse than not knowing how to warm up. If you don't leave them a blanket you risk finding them with coats on the bed in the morning. Tell them if there'll be enough hot water to have a bath or shower. If your flatmate, say, has to go to work in the morning and you and your guest do not, then you should warn your guest and request respect for the worker's bathroom and kitchen requirements. And if your flatmate has his own food supplies, or just one precious item, or needs the last of the milk before the milkman comes, make sure your guest realizes that.

10

WEDDINGS: THE BRIDE AND GROOM

There is an enormous amount of etiquette, tradition, custom and practice bound up in weddings. But it is *not* all written in stone or enshrined in law, and the world won't end if you change things round or don't do things the way your mother says you should. The legal requirements need to be checked on and the requirements of whoever is to conduct the service, but the only other essentials are the bride and groom, and a ring for the bride. Everything else is up for grabs.

Of course, most people want more than the minimum, and a lot of weddings share a lot of features – all I'm saying is that if you're getting married you shouldn't let yourself be bullied into doing anything you don't want to just because 'you have to have it' and 'everyone has it'. Neither of these things is probably true. The main reason for knowing what the traditions and customs are is so that you can choose which bits you want.

Getting Engaged
This is simply a decision by the two people concerned that they are going to marry. It has no legal status as such and generally involves two things: telling people and buying a ring.

The Engagement Ring
This is not essential, though most couples do like the symbolic aspect of it: there's something to show for the decision, a symbol of commitment. The man proposes (traditionally of course but

not essential – it is perfectly good manners for a woman to propose marriage; lots of couples these days 'sort of decided it together'), the woman accepts. After this, there are two schools of thought. Either he produces the ring from his back pocket or the couple wander off, arms entwined, to choose the ring together.

The back pocket is seen as frightfully romantic and perhaps the prerogative of old-fashioned and romantic men. Of course, it has its practical problems. What if the ring doesn't fit? What if she says 'No'? But these matters are not insuperable as a good jeweller will exchange for size and give money back. (The embarrassment of a man forced to tell the jeweller that she turned him down is something no etiquette book can help with.)

Going to choose together raises a couple of etiquette points. Before setting off, you should reach a clear agreement on who is paying and what is the price limit. Traditionally, the man always paid (it was one of the few wedding items he did pay for) but there is no reason why a couple can't share the cost of the ring. Most women would baulk at buying their own, even today, but if they like good jewellery – for example – they might like to make a contribution to get the best ring possible. If the man alone is paying, then he may feel embarrassed at imposing a budgetary restraint, but, of course, it has to be done. (If two people are going to get married, then they really are going to have to get used to talking about money anyway.) One possibility is for the man to go to the jewellers first and ask for a tray to be prepared in the right price range, from which his fiancée can pick.

Telling People

Traditionally, the two sets of parents should be told first. Couples who get engaged at the rugby club disco can't quite manage that but should tell parents as soon as possible. They should be told first because they are the people most likely to mind if they aren't (or even – heaven forbid – they hear it from someone else first). You should immediately tell anyone else who falls into this category – family, godparents, best friends.

You can put an announcement in the newspaper if this would be a good way of letting your particular circle know or it's a family custom, but it's not incorrect not to. Choose which paper you think appropriate and ring their classified ad department.

They can help and advise on wording. The classic formula goes something like this:

> *Montague/Campbell* A marriage has been arranged [or 'The engagement is announced'] between Robin, younger son of Mr and Mrs Richard Montague of Verona Street, London, and Julia, only daughter of Mr and Mrs Robert Campbell of Wood Lane, Eastleigh.

There are standard variations for use if any of the parties is divorced or widowed, and the newspaper will be able to advise you.

Modern Times

These days it is quite likely that a couple may live in one town and their respective families in two completely different places. Old rules about the groom's mother 'calling on' the bride's mother once the engagement was announced are not particularly helpful. Wherever you all live, the couple should take the initiative to try to ensure that all parties meet each other before the wedding. A visit to each set of parents is probably the minimum.

Asking Permission

A man is traditionally supposed to ask his bride's father for her hand in marriage. If he wants to do this, then fine, that's perfectly correct, but it is by no means necessary in this day and age. In fact there is a possible downside to it. Some fiancées might be offended, feeling they are being treated as a chattel. Or the bride's mother might feel she is entitled to be asked as well.

Who Runs It

Traditionally, the bride's parents 'give' the wedding: they organize it and pay for it, and the bride is married from their house. In a different age, the bride was assumed to be living at home until the day she was married, and so the arrangement worked quite well: she and her mother were supposed to spend the long winter evenings making plans, drawing up lists and embroidering her trousseau, ready for her June nuptials. Most people's lives don't look like that these days, even if the bride does live at home. But many couples do still get married from the bride's parents' home, even if she lives somewhere quite different – possibly even with the groom – and it's still a nice tradition.

Who Pays?
The usual thing is that the bride's parents pay for almost everything but you can change that if it feels right to you. If people want to contribute, then they should be allowed to, even if you think they really don't need to. Grown-up children might well feel they have more money than their parents, they've lived away from home, they should pay for the whole wedding. The parents may accept gratefully and breathe a sigh of relief. But you may also find that they have always counted on paying for your wedding, that they've even been saving for it, that they'd be proud and pleased to pay for it. In this case, it would be rude and hurtful to refuse. The best idea is obviously to share the costs: for instance, the groom's parents will often pay for the drinks at the reception.

Invitations
These are normally printed or engraved and go out about ten to twelve weeks before the day itself. Engraved is supposed to be better than printed and is tons more expensive. I don't think it matters a bit in this day and age, and, unless you are unbelievably rich, then it's probably a good idea to save your money and spend it on something with more tangible benefits, like food and drink.

You can buy pre-printed invitations, which you fill in yourself. Traditionalists may look askance but take no notice. You can write personal invitations to everyone if you like, though this is probably only practical for a small number of guests.

If you get them printed, then the firm will be able to advise you on wording and styles if you're not sure. They will have lots of sample invitations so you can get some idea of how they look.

The formal way is for the bride's parents to invite guests in the third person (i.e. they say, 'Mr and Mrs X request the pleasure . . .' rather than 'We'd like you to come to our daughter's wedding . . .'). This wording can be changed to reflect any other family circumstances – if one of the bride's parents is dead, or they are divorced, or other relations of the bride are hosting the wedding, or the engaged couple is giving the wedding. The invitations come from – logically – whoever is giving the wedding, and their names go on the top line, be they step-parent or the bride herself.

If the bride's parents *are* the hosts, this is the traditional wording:

Mr and Mrs James Smith
request the pleasure of your company
at the marriage of their daughter
Jane Anne
to
Mr John Alan Coombs
at 3 pm on Saturday 14th October
at St Peter's Church, Winchester
and afterwards at the Victoria Rooms, Hyde

RSVP
Egbert House
Hyde
Winchester

The guests' names will be written at the top of this invitation.

Evening-only Invitations
Many couples nowadays have the wedding service, then a meal immediately afterwards, then a party in the evening. In this case they may invite many more people to the party than they could afford to entertain to the meal. This is obviously a good idea if you have lots of workmates, say, and are on a low budget. This means that you have two invitations: one for the wedding and first reception, one for the second, and you send people either both or just the second one. You can buy pre-printed invitations for an evening wedding party too, and it may be sensible to buy these even if you're having the wedding invitations specially printed.

On the Day
Grooms are expected to be early at the church, and they should politely greet guests as they arrive. They don't need to do much else and are positively expected to look harassed and vague and not remember anyone's name.

Brides have no obligations up to the wedding except to panic and worry about their appearance and make everyone's life hell.

At the wedding the couple should try to make their responses loud and clear. Everything else is part of the service and not etiquette.

The Reception
Often starts with a receiving line. The bride, groom, the two sets of parents and, if you like, bridesmaids and best man, all line up and greet each arriving guest in turn. After this, the reception takes whatever form you want, though if guests sit down to eat – no matter how informally – then one table is reserved for the wedding party. Bride, groom, both sets of parents, best man and chief bridesmaid are seated there, along with whoever conducted the service if he or she comes (it is always polite to ask them – unless they're a family friend they may well refuse) and any particularly honoured or aged guest. Others can be seated there too, but going on the top table is not necessarily the summit of human aspirations: some people will see it as an honour and be delighted, but young people may well find it rather dull and would much rather be with friends their own age.

Talking to Guests
The bride and groom should try to circulate during the reception, after the meal and before the speeches. Wedding guests (polite ones) are sometimes wary of talking to the bride and groom, even if they're great friends, because they assume the new couple will have something much more important to do, or more important people to talk to, and they don't like to seem pushy. It is an excellent idea for the couple to go round all the other tables for a few minutes at a time (trying not to concentrate on those containing their own friends too much). Conversation will run on predictable lines (let's see the ring/wasn't the service nice/this food is lovely/were you nervous?) so it's very easy and pleasant and the whole thing will go some way to combat the view of bride and groom as some stuffed king and queen graciously looking out over their subjects.

Speeches
There is a traditional set order for this: father of the bride makes his speech, then proposes the toast to the new couple. Husband thanks father-in-law, makes own speech, then proposes toast on behalf of the lovely bridesmaids. Best man then says thank you on behalf of bridesmaids, makes own speech and sits down. He may also read out any messages.

You can follow the above format to the letter if you want, but you can change it too. No-one should be bullied by talk of 'the right thing'. If people hate speech-making, then they shouldn't be forced (though if the best man hates speech-making, then he's perhaps not a great choice).

After the Wedding

Of course the new couple must have a lovely honeymoon and live happily ever after. But *far more important than this*: they must write thank you letters for the presents. They must write them soon after the wedding and they must try to fill at least a side of notepaper.

It is normally the bride who writes, but there is no reason why the husband shouldn't write some or all, or they each write some of each letter. Keep a copy of your list of wedding guests handy when opening presents. You can write down what each gift is against the name, and then tick them off when you've written the thank you.

The thank you should mention what the gift was (to show you know which one it was), say that you're really pleased with it (giving some special reason if you can – it's the right colour for your bedroom, you both love waffles, you've always admired Picasso), thank them for coming to the wedding (or regret they couldn't make it), and perhaps add a bit about the honeymoon or going back to work. That will easily fill a side of paper, and you could still add how much you both enjoyed the wedding, how much you liked meeting their new boyfriend, you hope to see them soon, you hope they'll come over and let you cook them dinner using your new pans. The letter doesn't have to be terribly original – everyone always does say the same things about weddings – but it does have to sound reasonably personal. You can write very similar letters to everyone, but make sure there's something that is just for this recipient. It's a doddle really, just time-consuming. But you must do it. No excuses.

If some people couldn't come to the wedding, and you think they'd appreciate it – perhaps elderly relatives – you could send them a photo of the happy event and a slice of wedding cake. You could include these in the thank you letter if they sent presents anyway.

You should be sure to write thank yous to everyone who helped in any way, even if they were paid – clergyman, musicians, whoever did the flowers. Again, send cake if appropriate.

If friends give money as a present, then in your thank you letter you should say what you intend to spend the money on. You aren't on oath on this but, if you tell everybody you're going to buy a sofa, you'd better produce one sooner or later: and, if you tell several separate friends that you bought a kettle with their money, you'd better not invite them all round at once and have them each claim this appliance as their gift.

11

WEDDINGS: CLASS, PRESENTS AND OTHER DIFFICULTIES

If You Think You Are Marrying Someone of a Much Higher or Lower Social Class than Yourself
For simplicity's sake, I shall deal with this problem as if it centred only on disparity of income. Of course, that isn't all – it may not even be the major consideration – but the terms 'rich' and 'poor' can be used to describe the two sides.

There are a few points to remember. The first is this: in general, whoever is paying for the wedding gets to set the tone. If the bride is marrying someone who – for ease – I will describe as much richer than she, and her parents are paying, then her parents' ways will prevail. Their modest tastes (if that is what they are), their choice of caterer, their down-market relatives (if that is how they will be seen). If, on the other hand, she is the daughter of 'Money', then her parents can spend as much as they want, and his family might well murmur that they'd rather have had something less formal, but then it is not for them to say.

If the bride is poorer, the groom's family may offer to help financially. This should obviously be done tactfully, but if, say, the groom's family wants to invite large numbers of relatives to the wedding, then it is also only fair. Of course, anyone paying gets some say in the arrangements, but this should be sorted out by friendly discussion and negotiation. Compromise is the thing to look for.

It is always worth remembering that polite good-natured people at all income levels don't judge people on money standards. If you feel someone else is looking down on you, then that person is not worth worrying about.

If you consider you're marrying into a higher class and you're worried about your own behaviour with your new in-laws, then the rest of this book will help you (in particular, the section on Class). Good basic manners will take you everywhere from palace to hovel, and you should practise them everywhere. It would be very bad, after all, to treat your mother-in-law more politely than your own mother. Polite people make a good impression anywhere, and they treat everyone the same.

Your beloved should be able to help – always ask him or her first to explain things. He should be sensitive to your problems. If he's not, it could well be because he knows how unimportant it is if you get things wrong. If he does something terrible like repeating your low-voiced question about napkins to a whole tableful of relations, then tackle him afterwards. Say, 'You know how nervous I am, please don't do that in front of your mother, I want her to like me.'

Don't be shy. Try to get into conversation with your in-laws. Ask them about themselves or about your partner – that should be a topic that interests you all. If asked about yourself, don't boast too much (unattractive) but no harm in showing yourself in a good light. If asked about your own family and background, then you shouldn't lie, but needn't go into too much detail if you don't want to.

Presents

Wedding Lists
A lot of couples do produce a list of suggestions for wedding presents and if you're happy with the idea – you think it saves duplication and your friends and family seem to want one – then fine. If you find the idea tasteless and embarrassing, then there is no need to provide one.

Money as a Gift
Different cultures have different attitudes to money as a gift. For many people, money from wedding guests is welcome and expected, and there is a time set aside during the wedding for handing over these gifts. If this is your culture, then fine; you (or your family) know the rules. But in traditional British life, this is not the case. People do give money as a present, but the bridal couple should not ask for it.

About Presents Generally
Although you know perfectly well you're going to get lots and lots of them, you should still act surprised and pleased. You should *never* look as though you're soliciting them. People say, 'It's ridiculous to pretend: I know perfectly well people will bring them, and they know too, so why shouldn't I tell them what I want?' 'Because it's rude,' is why not. So no sending out lists unasked.

Second Marriages
The general rule is that these are more informal and relaxed. They are significantly less likely to happen in a church, which for a start cuts down on most people's more grandiose plans. Many couples marrying for a second time don't want presents, but guests who would like to give something could always go for a token bottle or something more on the birthday present lines (book, picture, CD) or useful-cheap-and-pretty items like stationery, photo albums or frames, or candles.

If only one of the partners has been married before, the other – or their family – may not want to be done out of a proper wedding. This is particularly likely if the first-timer is the woman. A little tactful accommodating is all that's needed here. Weddings in general (unless you're very lucky and friendly) tend to divide into the two separate sides very quickly – not necessarily in a combative way – and this is actually a useful feature of this kind of wedding. The new partner's side can act like it's a traditional wedding in every respect, while the old hand's side can giggle in corners about past history. Their cavalier attitude to the wedding – particularly if they are even tempted to imply that this marriage might not last either – must be kept to themselves. Care must be taken not to speak too loudly and particularly not to hurt the feelings of, or worry, the new bride's mother (she's probably worried enough on her own account, thank you).

Calling off a Wedding
I am glad to say I do not have to consider the emotional implications or the rights and wrongs of this. Whenever and whyever it has happened, this is what you must do.

If the decision is not mutual, then you must tell your partner as soon as possible that you are not going to marry him or her. This may seem obvious, but people lose their nerve and put it off, even when they're really sure they've made up their minds. It is bad enough to be jilted before a marriage, but even worse if you soon realize that everyone, absolutely everyone, knew before you did because your intended discussed it with them all at great length. Breaking an engagement is a sad fact of life: treating the jilted one so badly is very, very bad manners.

Telling People
The next thing to do is to tell everyone else, and as quickly as possible. You may find this very embarrassing, but you must not use that as an excuse for dithering. Close relatives or friends may volunteer to help and it's a good thing to let them: it will be less embarrassing for everyone if they don't hear the news direct from the bride and groom. (Apart from anything else, disappointed guests can ask a few more discreet questions of the bride's friend than of the bride.)

The best thing is to use all the lists you have prepared for the wedding. Go through the guest list one by one, and then cancel the arrangements for the flowers, caterers, church, photographers. If you are too hysterical to think about things, then calm down long enough to make very sure someone else is going to be practical. First of all, it's only polite: guests make expensive and elaborate arrangements to attend a wedding. The sooner you tell them it's off, the less put out they will be. And people you employ for the wedding will not only be put out if you forget to tell them and they turn up on the day, they will also charge you, and are fully entitled to do so. If you call off very soon before the wedding you may well lose deposits or even more. This can't be helped and you might as well accept it: it costs money to cancel any big event.

If you can't face phoning them you can try writing. The correct format for an announcement is this:

The marriage arranged between Miss Jane Smith and Mr Robert Browning will not now take place.

If your engagement was announced in the newspaper, you may like to put this announcement in the paper. People do. There is no necessity if you think it harrowing and humiliating, and you cannot assume that everyone will see it: you must still contact all guests separately.

The Engagement Ring
The rules here are very simple. Assuming the groom paid for the ring, if the bride calls off the wedding she must give it back to

him. If he is the one to break the engagement, then she is entitled to keep it, if she wants it. (It is also perfectly correct to give it back to him icily or throw it in his face even. Or throw it in the river in front of him.)

If the cost was shared, then they must reach agreement on either selling it (or returning it if the jeweller is understanding) and splitting the proceeds, or on one party buying out the other. Again, there is nothing to stop one party saying, 'Please, you have it,' either out of generosity or an attempt to induce guilt.

The same is true of any goods bought together by the couple, from a house downwards.

Presents

All presents (engagement presents and any wedding presents) should be returned,. What the bride should NOT do is say to people, 'Do you want your present back?' because many guests will hesitate to say, 'Yes, I do actually,' especially to someone who has perhaps been having a hard time. But they should say, 'Yes.' The bride should have said, 'Here is your present – thank you very much for having thought of us, I'm so sorry this has all happened, and I hope the shop will take it back.'

A wedding present is exactly that: if the wedding doesn't take place, then there is no justification for the couple keeping the goods. Even if the gift is not much use to the guest, he can always keep it for another wedding.

There is sometimes a vague assumption that some marriage or other will take place some time, so the present will cover that, but the fact is that the guest, if invited a second time, will usually feel that he has to buy something new, if only to save embarrassment with the new partner – 'Perhaps you don't know that I gave your fiancée that coffee machine she's been using for the past two years so even if it's broken now and you're unlikely to get much benefit – well, it's my wedding present to you.'

Postponement

If a marriage is being postponed, perhaps because a parent of one of the couple has died, then the procedure is similar to that outlined above, substituting 'postponed' for 'called off' and adding a sentence of explanation.

If there is a death in the near family, then it is up to the couple and their families to decide what to do, and probably specifically the bride and her mother. If a large, elaborate wedding has been organized, and a day or two beforehand a relative outside the immediate family dies, then few brides would be blamed for going ahead. The same applies if the relative or friend was very old, or had been ill a long time. They may sound heartless, but life does have to go on, and marriages are as important a part of life as deaths are, and have their own priority. However, saying, 'It's what Granny would have wanted,' is pretty tacky. Leave it to people to think it out for themselves.

If the death is someone closer – parent or sibling perhaps – then there are two choices: postpone the wedding, or go ahead but without any major celebrations (i.e. without most of the guests, and with only a simple meal or very small reception for immediate family afterwards). Both these choices are irreproach-able. If the bride wants to go ahead with the full wedding anyway, then there is nothing to stop her doing so – she will certainly be criticized, but she may well not care a bit. If, for example, she was not very fond of whoever died she may even think it would be hypocritical to call the wedding off. It's up to her. Either partner, however, should be careful about assuming that a death in the other family can't be important enough to matter: he or she may be surprised to find out what his or her partner thinks.

12

ATTENDANTS AT THE WEDDING

All participants in the wedding party are chosen by the bride and groom.

Attendants have two main jobs: (1) be supportive and (2) do what you're told.

The Best Man

Being a best man is quite a serious, responsible post. You are expected to have some control over the groom, and you are supposed to make sure that he turns up on time, dressed correctly, ring in hand. The groom is forgiven for all kinds of little errors and lapses (nerves, you see) but the best man is judged by higher standards. He must organize the groom's side properly, sort out the ushers, and take charge in the church. He is often one of the two official witnesses to the ceremony who sign the register.

His next job is to try to ensure that everyone has transport to the reception and knows where to go.

At the reception he will probably have to organize the speeches after the meal, and then make a speech. There is some tradition of vulgarity in the best man's speech, but this is best avoided. Nobody should be offended by his speech. I think the ideal for the best man is that he reveal some fact about the bridegroom which is fascinating for the guests (particularly those on the bride's side who may not know him well), embarrassing for the groom, but morally irreproachable. Star example: the best man who revealed that as a child the groom had appeared on children's television in a game show, and won. The best man is traditionally expected to tell a joke or funny story: this should preferably be relevant but clean.

The best man will be told what he has to wear: either morning dress or dark business suit normally.

The groom is expected to thank the best man with a bottle of whisky and a pair of cufflinks.

The Ushers

Their main responsibility is to help the best man in the church: handing out service sheets, directing people where to sit, giving a helping arm to elderly relations. Friends and relations of the bride sit on the left-hand side of the church (facing the altar), while the groom's connections sit on the right.

If the other main men in the wedding are in morning suits (see Fig. 8 overleaf), then so will the ushers be. Otherwise they dress as the other male guests, in their best suits. In that case the role of usher is considerably more informal (as no-one can tell who is and who isn't) and all potentially helpful and able-bodied males can be drawn into the fold. The ushers should be chosen from both sides at the wedding, so there is a good chance that guests will be recognized by someone or other, and the bride's favourite aunt will be sure she is at the correct wedding.

The ushers, if in morning dress, will be expected to participate in a foolish group photo for all those with top hats. They are expected to look young and devil-may-care in this picture, throwing their hats in the air or wearing them at a silly angle. They should then help the best man with directing guests to the reception. They can help by bringing their own cars if they have them and offering lifts to lost-looking uncles as well as pretty young female guests. That is the end of their duties: they may now enjoy the reception.

They are generally thanked with a bottle of sherry from the happy couple.

The Bridesmaids

It is not essential to have any. If there are none, people think the bride didn't want to have any attention distracted away from her as she walked up the aisle. But it's a perfectly reasonable decision not to have any, particularly if the other choices are ten brides-maids or a terrible family rift.

Bridesmaids are given flowers to carry, supplied by the bride's family. They wear what they are told (although all good brides

Fig. 8. Formal morning attire for men.

will have considered their feelings). They are traditionally thanked with a gift of a silver bracelet or necklace (which junior bridesmaids are supposed to keep for best but take to school on Monday to show off and lose).

Chief Bridesmaid/Matron of Honour

The same role, but described by the second name if she is already married herself. Usually the bride's best friend or closest sister. There is no age limit on bridesmaids, and the bride should pick whomever she feels will best fulfil the role, but an older bridesmaid's costume should be appropriate.

On the day, the chief bridesmaid keeps any younger maids in line, arranges the bride's train, if any, and takes her bouquet when the exigencies of the service mean she needs her hands free.

During the ceremony and photographs, she checks the bride is OK, pulls and tugs to straighten the dress and veil from time to time, murmurs encouragement, tries to ensure no-one is standing on the hem of the dress, and keeps saying, 'You look great.' She is often one of the official witnesses to the wedding and so signs the register.

13

HOW TO BE A GOOD
WEDDING GUEST

The Invitation
You can answer in one of two ways:

Formal
Miss Kim Ward thanks Mr and Mrs Howard Purnell for their
kind invitation to the wedding of their daughter Rachel on 3rd
September [at Lord Have Mercy Church at 3 pm: this bit can be
omitted if you like] and is pleased to be able to accept.

For a refusal: Miss Kim Ward thanks Mr and Mrs Howard
Purnell for their kind invitation to the wedding of their daughter Rachel, and regrets very much that she will not be able to
attend, owing to a prior engagement/illness in the family/deep
mourning.

Informal
An informal reply implies only that it is not in the third
person: it is still a proper polite letter. It may be more
appropriate: (a) if you want to impart more information or
details; (b) you feel it suits your personal style better, and that
you'd feel ridiculous and unfriendly writing in the third
person; or (c) if you know the people who issued the
invitation quite well.

Dear Mr and Mrs Purnell,
    Thank you so much for your kind invitation to Rachel and Tim's wedding on 3rd September. I'm delighted to be able to accept and I look forward to meeting you then. [Or: I look forward to seeing you then, if you know them.]

                    Yours sincerely,

                    Kim Ward

    Refusal:

Dear Mr and Mrs Purnell,
    Thank you so much for your kind invitation to Rachel and Tim's wedding on 3rd September. I very much regret [or: I am very disappointed] that I shan't be able to come. Unfortunately, I have a long-standing family engagement on that day. I'm sure you'll all have a marvellous day though, and please tell Rachel and Tim I'll be thinking of them.

                    Yours sincerely,

                    Kim Ward

There is no need to go into enormous detail, but if the couple are close friends you may wish to make it clear that it is something important which is keeping you away.
    If a couple has been invited and only one can come, then an informal letter is probably the only way to reply: '. . . I shall be delighted to attend, but unfortunately Robin will be away on a business trip on that day so can't come. He sends his apologies and regrets.' Traditionally, it was always assumed that invitations to couples were handled and answered by the woman, and, if that suits you, then fine, but there is no reason why the man shouldn't answer invitations.
    If you are single and have been invited alone, then you can't bring your partner of the moment, nor can you, really, ask to bring him or her, unless you're very sure your bride (a) won't mind you asking and (b) would feel able to say 'no' if she wanted to.
    If you are married, engaged or living with someone, then you generally assume that your partner is going to be invited with

you. If both names are not on the invitation, then you probably need to ask, especially if your friends may not know your current situation. 'Do you want me to bring John, my husband/fiancé/partner?' is polite in these circumstances.

What to Wear

I'm dealing here with traditional British society and religions. If you are of a different culture, then you will have your own rules which you or your family know. If you are going to a wedding in a different culture, then the only thing is to ask whoever is your main contact with the wedding: bride, groom or parent. As a visitor you would probably be expected to conform to your own standards: i.e. wear what you would wear to a smart wedding in your own culture. If there are special arrangements for, say, headgear or footwear, then you will be told, or *ad hoc* arrangements will be available at the wedding.

At any wedding, the really important thing is *to look as though you have made an effort*. The effort may have been to iron your frock, or to wear a tie, but that is what matters. Most guests will wear a smart outfit: best suit for men, dress or suit for women. (Hats are not essential for women guests: if you love to wear them, then make the most; if you don't, then don't.) But if the smartest you can manage is sports jacket, good trousers, shirt and tie, or if you can't afford a new dress, but you take something old and pretty and iron it carefully and polish your shoes, then that's fine. It is the effort that counts, and it is that which shows.

Traditionally, female guests do not wear either black or white for weddings. This has eased a lot, and certainly you shouldn't worry if part of your outfit is one of these colours – nobody objects nowadays (as they once did) to a black hat or a white skirt.

Presents

You can ask if there is a list, if that suits you (if you choose something from it you should inform whoever is running the list to avoid duplication).

You should spend what you want on a present. Old clichés are true: a small cheap present bought with care and thought, or something you've made, is just as good as an expensive gift. If you can only afford a token present, that's fine.

In the past it was considered incorrect to bring wedding

presents to the service itself. The correct thing was to deliver them, or have them delivered or sent to the bride's mother's house (which in those days, of course, was also assumed to be the bride's house). It was seen as inconsiderate to bring them to the wedding because someone would have to look after them.

Nowadays this has quite gone by the board. It is still perfectly correct to deliver or send them early, but it is now so common for people to bring presents to the reception that arrangements will have been made for them (usually a member of the catering staff will offer to relieve you of the parcel, or you will easily spot a table set aside for presents) so you need have no qualms.

If you are feeling kind, you can include the receipt for your gift so that your friends can exchange it if it's a duplicate. The easy way to do this is to put the receipt in an envelope, seal it, then write on the outside: 'Receipt and one-year guarantee for travel kettle, from Jane and Dave.'

If you want to give money, then write a short note and put it with a cheque or a banknote in an envelope. The couple should, sooner or later, give you some imaginative destination for your money – a nice vase, we hope, rather than the electricity bill or the fourth evening meal on their honeymoon.

On the Day

Good guests join in all the hymns and don't make a nuisance of themselves if they're taking photos or videoing the ceremony. It is a lost cause to expect them not to throw confetti, no matter how many notices there are up in the church.

Parents control their small children throughout wedding and reception, keeping them reasonably quiet, stopping them from running around and removing them if they get too difficult.

At the reception, guests don't get drunk, and they keep their voices down. Naturally they will want to discuss the service, the other side, and the past history of bride and groom. But they should try to make sure their comments are confined to their own groups and not shouted to the unwilling edification of the table of aunts next door.

They have a duty to be friendly and polite to the new people they meet at the wedding, but they do not have an obligation to circulate widely and go round making friends. Young single people do this because they like to: but older guests who see the wedding as an opportunity to catch up on the news with a group of old friends should be allowed to do so and should not be forced to mingle with a group of people they will never meet again.

Further to this, be careful what you say to chance-met fellow guests at weddings: don't make any critical remarks about anyone (you know whose son they will turn out to be!) and be careful, for example, what you say about the bride and groom's past lives, or even current lives. Not everyone may know that they're already living together, or that one has been married before. However hypocritical this may seem to you, it is not your business to inform people.

If there is a receiving line, be ready to introduce yourself and your companion, if any, as briefly as possible. No need to go into great or embarrassing detail, 'I'm a friend of Daisy's' will do, even if you are the sister of her first husband, or 'I'm Paul's cousin' even if you're his step-sister's second cousin once removed. The bride is resigned to being kissed by just about everyone, so do so if you wish. Traditionally, you say, 'Congratulations' to the groom and 'Good luck' to the bride. This does still hold, though lots of people wouldn't notice. To everyone else you say, 'Hello' or 'Delighted to meet you' – more if you want. Anyone can be told how good he looks, and that it was a lovely service, and isn't it a wonderful moment, and wasn't it lucky/a shame about the weather. But the point of the receiving line is that you go through it as fast as you can.

Wedding Cake
Anyone who sleeps with wedding cake under her pillow will dream of her future spouse, so it's important to bring some home with you to offer to your single-and-proud-of-it flatmates or siblings and irritate them to death. There will probably be attractive silver-printed wedding napkins to wrap it up in, which will not, however, prove greaseproof, and the cake will leave a nice stain inside your smartest bag or the pocket of your best suit.

The End of the Reception
Guests should not play tricks on the departing couple, and all sensible couples will do their best to preclude any pranks. A little bit of decoration of the car is just about permissible – anything on the lines of joke phone calls to honeymoon hotels is completely out, and very bad manners.

Single female guests are expected to stand around as the bride is leaving and have the bouquet thrown at them (whoever catches it is the next to get married).

Stag and Hen Nights

What exactly these consist of is not, I am glad to say, a subject for an etiquette book. But whether your choice is an elegant ladies' supper or a pub crawl with strippers, there is one vital rule: don't hold them the night before the wedding. The weekend before is usually a good time. The other rule is that anything said or done at them should be forgotten later, or (if that's not possible) they should be disinterred for discussion only in the presence of those who were there. It may be as well if the other half of the bridal couple, in particular, receives only the most rudimentary account.

Workmates and Weddings

Most people probably can't invite all their workmates, but colleagues are bound to hear a lot about the plans, so engaged couples should keep stressing their tight budget, tiny guest list, and decision to get married 200 miles away from where they work.

Workmates, even if not invited, will often club together to buy the couple a present and give them a card. It would be nice if in gratitude the bride or groom-to-be brought along their partner to meet the colleagues one lunchtime or evening, and bought everyone a drink in the pub next door, or brought a couple of bottles into the office – whatever seems most appropriate. A letter of thanks must, naturally, be sent to the office mates afterwards.

The bridal couple could also spare some cake to be brought into the office after the honeymoon. A small number of photos of the event will probably be very popular. A large number will not. And now the boss is standing there, tapping his watch and saying it's time for you all to get back to work and to normal life after that distraction . . .

PART TWO
EVERYDAY LIFE

14

HOW TO GET ON WITH THE PEOPLE YOU LIVE WITH

Whomever You Live With

Parents, children, lovers, friends – you should observe normal everyday politeness, saying 'Hello' and 'Goodbye' and 'Thank you'. You should keep each other up to date with basic information about your lives, and particularly about anything affecting the way you live together. Nobody should use up communal resources without replacing them, and you should take turns at doing awful jobs. I hope that you would do each other occasional favours, e.g. lending food when it runs out, that you would take messages for them, chat politely to their friends or relations on the phone or while waiting for them to emerge or return.

It seems to me only sensible that whomever you live with, and however old or young you or they are, you in general tell them if you're going out. There's no need to give details if you don't want to, or if they're secret or private, but everyone should be able to poke his head round the door and say, 'I'm off out now – I'm going to the pictures,' or 'I don't know if I'll be back tonight, so good luck for tomorrow.' Apart from anything else, it's a simple security measure – if you don't turn up when you should, then flatmates/parents can take appropriate action.

Sharing with Flatmates

Etiquette here requires only the basic politeness, as above. Other than that, it's up to you to work out your arrangements with the other sharers. Some people like to cook and eat together every evening and others don't. Some flats are always full of friends and relations sleeping on the floor or the sofa: other sharers don't like that kind of thing. Neither is right or wrong. All that matters is that you both agree.

Money

If you share bills, or one person is responsible for collecting and paying the rent, then it is extremely important that the other flatmates pay up on time and without moaning. It's one thing to run up your own debts, quite another to do it on someone else's behalf, especially if that person ends up paying your share out of his or her own pocket while waiting for your long-delayed cheque. And vague grumbling about your financial position and the size of the bills may seem reasonable to you, but is most unfair on someone who is merely passing your hard-earned and begrudged money on to someone else.

The Phone

You should do your best over phone messages. Often one flatmate thinks he does more than his fair share of answering the phone and writing messages, and if you think that, you can take it up with your friend, but you shouldn't leave her to find out you're not happy by her not getting an important message. Keep a notebook by the phone with a pen tied to it so it's always easy to write them down and find them. Agree a place where you leave messages for each other, or chaos will result.

You shouldn't really ask other people to lie for you on the phone: most flatmates are happy with the odd minor deception of the 'She's not in' variety, but beyond that you're putting too much responsibility on others. The most you can ask is that they continually say they don't know what you're up to. However, on general security grounds you shouldn't give out lots of information about your female flatmates (or yourself) to unknown people over the phone. (Even if you know them, you might ponder whether you're sure that your flatmate's boss needs to be told that she has gone out with her boyfriend and won't be back tonight.) It's surprising how people will blithely describe their and their friend's engagements to someone they don't know: 'She's not in, you can try again later but there may be no-one in after nine,' or 'No, there's just me here all evening,' are not advised, for various reasons. Of course, most people who phone will be harmless and real friends, but unfortunately in today's world you have to consider the one in a thousand who mightn't be. Never give more than minimal information unless you're very sure what you're doing.

For more on phones and security, see pages 117 and 168.

Confidentiality

Of course, polite people always keep secrets and don't gossip (very much), but you have a special duty to people that you live with. Without at all trying, you are bound to find out *something* about the people you live with that is really none of your business, and that you wouldn't have found out any other way: it might be financial, sexual, something about their appearance or health. The only thing to do is to forget you ever knew, no matter how interesting it is. If your flatmate wants to discuss it with you, fine, but you shouldn't tell other people unless you're very sure your flatmate wouldn't mind. Secrets found out about workmates or casual friends can be seen as fair game, but secrets about co-residents must be sacrosanct. It doesn't matter whether you've found out that he dyes his hair or that she had an illegitimate child adopted; if you wouldn't have known if you didn't share the flat, then you don't tell anyone. One good reason for this, apart from high-mindedness and natural justice, is that there's sure to be something he or she is going to find out about you one day. You'll feel happier if you accept this principle.

Borrowing and Lending

Don't ask to borrow something unless you're sure that the owner either won't mind lending it or won't mind refusing you. If someone does turn down your request, then you shouldn't take offence: no-one is obliged to do you favours, and there may be all kinds of good reasons to have refused you. Borrowers assume it is just meanness when lenders refuse, but this is not so. They may have rules about lending, or they may need the item you want to borrow. You may also be a person who tends not to return items. Lots of people, for some reason, think it perfectly all right to borrow books and not return them – a very maddening habit. People who are subject to persistent borrowings may eventually (rather unworthily) feel, 'Well, why don't you ever buy anything yourself?' If your friend regularly buys all the latest books or CDs and you catch yourself thinking, 'I needn't bother buying that, she'll have it,' then your actions may need urgent reviewing.

When borrowing and lending are free swaps to help each other out, practised equally by both sides (such as is often the case with female flatmates lending each other clothes, or with literature fans swapping their treasured books), then that it is fine. But anything that gets more one-sided is usually, quite frankly, an attempt by one party to save money at the expense of another. Even if you are invited and encouraged to borrow freely from the resources of someone who has many more dresses or books than you, it would be nice from time to time to express your gratitude and make it clear that you are aware that you are very favoured and lucky to have such an opportunity.

Of course, all items must be returned promptly and in good condition. You should not reduce your friends to the embarrassment of scouring your bookshelves and saying, 'Isn't that mine?' And if they do, saying, 'I've no idea – if it is yours, do take it,' is not reassuring to the lender.

Lending CDs
Some people borrow CDs or videos to copy them. This is illegal: you are stealing from the copyright holders of those recordings. If the owner of the CD refuses to allow you to do this, he is not only justified but also correct. (You might also wonder why he should be willing to give you for free what he had to pay for.)

Lending Clothes
If you are lent clothes, then you must wash or dry-clean them, and quickly. The old get-out, 'I wasn't sure what you'd want doing with it – it looks so fragile I didn't dare wash it myself,' is not good enough. Read the label, and, if there is the slightest doubt, then either hand-wash with enormous care or pay out for dry-cleaning. If it is damaged and you can't repair it, then you must own up and insist on replacing it. Don't ever think you can get away with just handing it back and saying nothing, and pretending innocence if asked later. This is horribly bad etiquette, and gets you nowhere anyway – no-one is going to be fooled.

Borrowing and Lending Money
This is an even stickier subject. Where large sums of money are involved, then you must try to be businesslike about it, but I should warn you that such transactions are still likely to be fatal to friendships. Be very sure what you are doing, and always consider the worst scenario: 'Suppose he never pays me back/I

can't pay her back? How will he and I feel about that?' Much better, if you possibly can (even if it is more trouble and more expensive), to borrow from a bank, who won't take it personally and which will still be able to pay its own rent if you're late with the repayments.

With smaller sums – a tenner till the weekend – you should keep an eye out for what you're doing. You may be vague about such sums, possibly forgetting to pay back but also forgetting to ask for them, and so it all evens out in the end. You think. But others might not see it that way at all. They might be wrong of course – lots of people find it easier to remember who owes them money than whom they owe to – but it's better to get these things sorted out. In fact, small transactions like this were more common and more forgivable in the past, before ATMs became so widespread. Then, if you'd missed the bank by 3.30 pm Friday, you'd had it for cash until Monday. This is far from true for most people nowadays: if you find yourself frequently cashless and borrowing (no matter how careful you are about paying back) you should perhaps re-consider your arrangements: to put it brutally, you are inconveniencing other people to support your own inefficiency.

It's important with your friends to establish an ambience where you and they can politely remind one another of debts, making a joke of it if necessary. People get too embarrassed to say anything which – with right-minded and well-meaning people – can lead to orgies of further embarrassment and horror: 'Why didn't you remind me? I feel dreadful.' 'I didn't like to – it's OK,' and so on. Much easier if everyone is in the habit of remembering and reminding.

15

WORK

Working environments vary so much in formality that it's very hard to lay down rules as to what's right and what's wrong. But some basic everyday etiquette points are standard.

Be polite to your fellow workers in saying, 'Hello,' and 'Goodnight,' first and last thing. If you're terribly busy rushing through corridors and keep meeting people, then it's fine to give them just a smile and nod after the first time that day. If someone wants to stop and talk and you have no time, it is very reasonable to interrupt as politely as possible and say, 'I'm terribly sorry, may I catch you later? I have to do this right now.' And of course you must be understanding if people do that to you.

People will normally tell you what they want you to call them, and you should follow what they say even if your personal preference would be for more formality or informality. If in doubt, always be more formal – Mrs Smith, Dr Bennett – until invited to use a Christian name.

Starting a New Job
You should be friendly and pleasant with everyone but don't start allying yourself with special groups or specific people too quickly. There may be all kinds of factions and undercurrents that you don't know about, and you could end up on the wrong side or with people you're really not in sympathy with. Be pleasant to everyone. If you are invited out for lunch or a drink by co-workers, then by all means go (if you want to) but don't find yourself in a regular arrangement too quickly. Listen carefully and pick up what you can about the office politics, and learn as much as you can about the chains of command in the

organisation. Identify quickly people who will answer your panic-stricken questions about your job. Be very cautious about listening to or joining in with any attacks on co-workers (except, possibly, attacks on those a long way above you).

Of course most of the fun and interest of a working life consists of the things I seem to be banning here: but all I'm suggesting is that you start slowly. You can throw yourself into it heart and soul when you know what you're doing and who the right people are.

Clothes

What to wear for work can only be judged from experience: wear a smart suit (men and women) or dress (women) the first day and take it from there. In general, if your job involves representing your company face-to-face to the general public (receptionist, sales rep), then high, and probably clearly specified, standards of formal dress will be expected. Those who burrow in offices or talk on telephones all day can be more casual.

Fig. 9. Dress smartly on your first day at work.

Taking Messages in the Office

If you are asked for someone who isn't there, then you must say, 'I'm afraid she isn't here at the moment. Is there anyone else who can help you, or can I take a message?'

You should be very careful about giving out any other information. If the caller asks for more, then you could say if you knew the person to be ill, or that he won't be back in the office this morning, but no more than that. It is perfectly all right to keep saying, 'I'm afraid I don't know,' or 'I'm afraid I can't tell you that.' Don't ever give personal information – 'She's at the ante-natal clinic' – or say, 'He's gone to the gents,' or 'She isn't back from lunch yet.'

Always leave a clear message for another person: date and time, and name of the person calling. When taking a message, you can ask the caller to repeat everything as often as is necessary, and to spell anything you're not clear about. This can feel tiresome and embarrassing, but it is not as bad as leaving an unhelpful or misleading message.

Male-Female Relations

Even women who demand very old-fashioned standards of etiquette from men in social life cannot expect the same at work. A man needn't rise when a woman enters a room in business unless the situation demands it and he would do the same for a man. Men and women should shake hands as equals, and whoever is most conveniently placed should open doors. Men, on the other hand, should not automatically expect a woman to make coffee or take minutes in meetings if it is not specifically her job.

Lots of people enjoy flirty but harmless relations with colleagues of the opposite sex, with nobody taking it seriously or being bothered or upset by it. But this can be a thorny area, and everybody should be careful. It's probably best to avoid flirtatious conversation in a work environment unless you're very sure what you're doing. Women subjected to sexual remarks or innuendo that they don't want should respond with a frown, a look of incomprehension or a look of contempt.

If accepting an invitation from a colleague or work contact, then make quite sure that you are both clear that this is strictly business, if it is. Don't accept if you think the other party hopes to combine it with pleasure and you're not interested. You won't enjoy yourself and you probably won't get far with work either.

Sexual Harassment

Men should beware of making overt remarks to women junior to them: these women may well not like it but feel unable to say so. This is at best bullying, and at worst sexual harassment. Women faced with this – a very real problem for those caught up in it, despite the wish amongst many people to call it a joke – should not be too embarrassed to take action against the harasser, preferably with the help of a more senior woman colleague.

You could try first to have a private talk with the man explaining your problem as calmly and politely as you can. Don't persevere if his responses show it isn't worth it, but occasionally it can work with someone who is just thoughtless and insensitive. Here it's worthwhile being tactful. This worked for me once: 'You probably don't realize that it can be quite difficult for a woman in this office, and I'm sure you mean only to be complimentary, but it makes life embarrassing and difficult for me when you make these remarks. I'm sure you didn't mean to upset me, etc., etc.' (You may well feel that you shouldn't have to be so conciliatory and careful of his feelings, and you're probably right, but I'm thinking of a situation where you value your job, don't want to cause a fuss, and know you will have to go on working with the harasser afterwards. It could be worth compromising if the job is worth it.)

Office Social Life

Of course, all should pay for their own drinks and meals in any kind of jollifications. Slight exceptions may be made if there is a wide range of seniority present: junior staff may accept drinks or help with the bill from more senior. However, this is income-related, not gender-related. It may be the case in most offices that poorer-paid staff are mostly female, but it's the intent that counts here: paying for your secretary's drinks does not turn this into a date and you cannot go on to treat her as a date.

Office Parties

Traditionally, everyone gets drunk, behaves very badly and it's all forgotten the next day. Getting drunk and behaving badly are never good etiquette, and you can be quite sure that nothing is forgotten.

For your first office party, you should check with other employees what the form is: if it's straight after work, do people change? Bring partners from outside? Bring bottles?

If you think you've behaved badly, then the best thing is to pretend on Monday that you don't remember a thing. Don't necessarily believe what people tell you about others being livid with you. Some people may have forgiven you anyway (or forgotten) and it may all be best left undisturbed – but watch out for pursed lips from former friends and apologize to them. If others have behaved badly, then you can kindly forget about it and say it doesn't matter, or you can make clear your displeasure and await developments.

Getting Jobs, Interviews

It definitely pays to remember your manners when applying for jobs and going for interviews. Politeness certainly does matter at these times. The process of applying for a job and going for an interview may give you the chance to demonstrate that you can write a polite letter, make and answer phone calls correctly and politely, make arrangements and stick to them, and greet people in a friendly and pleasant manner and talk politely to them. This will make a very favourable impression on prospective employers. Such simple manners give you an air of maturity and self-confidence, reassure your future boss that you could act as politely with clients and others and – you may be surprised to hear – are not, by any means, universal amongst job applicants.

16

PERSONAL SECURITY AND PRIVACY

This has already crept into various areas: it may not seem to have much to do with etiquette, but it has. Many of us are trapped between what we were taught was polite behaviour and the realities of the modern world. As children we were taught to act respectfully, politely and obediently to those older than us. But how are children to learn that if a polite man asks them to leave the park with him they must refuse?

As adults we can look after ourselves better (we hope) and we can spot dangerous situations. But still . . . lots of us don't like to be rude on the phone, and we put up with far too much. Total strangers ring up and we give them information. We are constantly asked about our personal circumstances, for all kinds of reasons, and we feel we must answer – we don't want to seem rude. For security reasons, or just for reasons of privacy, we may not want to answer, but we don't know how to get out of it.

Nosey Questions
There are two main rules to remember:

1. If strangers ask you questions, then you do not need to answer them if you don't want to, and it is not at all rude or impolite to refuse to do so. This includes people you don't know who phone you for any reason (even if they say they are a friend of a flatmate or mother) and people who serve you in shops, tell you they're doing an opinion poll, try to sell you something or are canvassing for a political party. (It is unfortunately true that just occasionally the

sneaky question-asker does turn out to be a friend of your mother's, but that is still her rudeness and not yours.)

You should refuse politely if you can or make an excuse if you wish: 'I can't tell you that,' or 'I don't know,' or 'I don't have the details you require,' or 'I'm afraid that's private.' If the other person persists, then you can get tougher. Don't be taken in by his looking or sounding hurt or upset or trying to imply that it is you who is being rude. *You are not.* Don't get involved in arguments about why you should tell him. It is not for you to justify yourself.

2.   If someone you know asks you questions, then you are also not obliged to answer if you don't want to. Here it is more important that you have some polite brush-off, but it is still not rude for you to refuse and it would be rude for the other person to press you.

If you think she shouldn't have asked the question ('How much do you earn?', 'Are you pregnant yet?', 'Are you and John faithful to each other?'), then I strongly recommend looking very shocked and saying, 'I can't believe you just asked me that,' and either leaving her to stumble out of it or moving on yourself to another, perhaps related, subject. If she tried to press you, as opposed to defending herself lamely and saying, 'I was just interested,' then you can keep the shocked look and say, 'I'm not telling you that,' with as much emphasis as you like on the 'you'.

But what if the question isn't quite so unforgivable? You don't want to answer it ('How much did you pay for that?', 'Are you sleeping with him?', 'Where did you buy that?' – these are strictly subjective examples by the way: you can decide for yourself what questions go into what categories). Or supposing the really awful question came from someone you don't feel you can be too hard on (elderly relative, boss). Then you need a more smiling response: 'I can't possibly tell you that,' or 'I'm not telling anyone that,' or 'Wouldn't you like to know?' or 'That's none of your business.' Any of these *if said with a cheerful face* should get you out of it. As ever, if people press, then they have lost the right to a polite answer.

There are questions that seem perfectly reasonable – 'Are you planning to move?', 'Are you going to go back to work?', 'Are you going on holiday this year?' – but if answered truthfully might lead to minefields or unexpected (and maybe unwanted) revelations of bankruptcy, pregnancy, redundancy, divorce, etc. Here you are free to tell white lies and say, 'We don't know/haven't decided yet/ haven't really thought about it.' Looking vague and serene and changing the subject is the key here. You generally find that people did leap to conclusions, but they were the wrong ones ('I was convinced that meant you were getting married, not splitting up,') and nothing to worry about. If the question was reasonable, then it's polite to embarrass the asker as little as possible – he was probably only making conversation in the first place.

Safety

Privacy and safety go together because you use one to help with the other. Some of this applies largely to women, but by no means all of it. In general, a lot of trouble can be avoided if you don't give out unnecessary information. For example, if you live on your own, there's no need to stress that to people you don't know. If you're going to be on holiday for a week and your flat will be empty, then don't tell the whole pub where you live (that is exactly how burglars pick up useful information). If your collection of stamps is valuable, then don't pass this information on routinely to absolutely everybody.

You may think these points are obvious, but I'm astonished at the number of conversations I hear when people are (apparently without concern) giving away this kind of information to groups of people in public places or over the telephone to virtual strangers. You can't imagine it? How about this: 'You need to measure up the kitchen to give me a quote – well, it'll have to be the week after next because I'm away until then. No, evening please, I'm out all day at work.' I'm not trying to promote a paranoid attitude, just one that's reasonably careful. Of course, most people aren't criminals and aren't out to get you, but it doesn't do any harm to be discreet.

Contacting People Through Dating Agencies, Websites and Newspaper Advertisements

In recent years, more and more people have been using the above media to meet people and arrange dates so I think a few extra words of caution are needed here. You should also follow any security advice given by the newspapers and websites.

If you place an advert, either in a newspaper or on a website, never include your phone number(s), home, work or email addresses. Instead use a box number or the equivalent facility offered by the website.

When you make contact with someone, never give out personal details (especially financial details) until you are sure that the person you are communicating with is genuine; certainly, never give anyone your home or work address until you have met him or her.

Never meet anyone until you have exchanged *landline* telephone numbers (not just mobile numbers) and have spoken at least three times by phone. A lunchtime date is preferable to an evening date for the first meeting. Always make your own travel arrangements, both to and from the meeting; don't accept a lift home on the first date. Meet at a public place that is well-known and convenient to you and tell a good friend where you are going, who you are meeting and when you will be back. Take your mobile phone with you and ring your friend during the meeting to confirm that everything is fine.

17

YOUNG CHILDREN

The gulf between proud parents and the childless is never greater than on visiting days. Thin-lipped single people sit watching as the child wreaks destruction. Parents think, 'Wait till she has children – then she'll see.' Let's try to call a truce and lay down a few rules for either side. And the first rule is that each side should read the section addressed to the other as well as their own, so they get a clear picture.

Addressed to the Childless

When Visiting Friends with Children
You're on their territory, so in politeness you accept their ways and standards. If your visit covers a time when the children are not in bed, then you owe them the same courtesy as everybody else in the household. You say 'Hello' and make as much conversation as you can. It's not very original to ask them how old they are and what they like about school, but they're probably used to it if you can't think of something better.

If the children want to climb on you, then you don't need to let them, but you must put them off politely. Having your good clothes on is a reasonable excuse, but if you are visiting a household with toddlers during the daytime (as opposed to coming to a dinner party in the evening only), then really you should adapt your outfit and not wear silk shirts and dry-clean-only sweaters.

If you want to bring the children presents, then that's polite and generous, but you should be sure to bring the right kind of thing. Lots of children nowadays are discouraged from eating sweets and you won't be popular with their parents if that's what you bring. Toy drums and other noisy items will also win the love of the children but not the adults. And beware of bringing something that's too old for the child. It may seem sophisticated and delightful to them, but it may also require a level of co-ordination not yet achieved, which will surely end in tears. I shudder to remember the bead-stringing set I bought a four year old: she loved it, but the whole family spent the weekend chasing the tiny beads which were all over the floor, rolling everywhere, easy to spill and impossible for tiny fingers to thread.

Parents are not usually open to much teasing about their children. Try to find something to compliment their offspring on ('How lively they are!'), and if you want to remove them, stop them going into your bag, stop having to read them stories, then you must try to word it nicely and not appear to be criticizing. But don't take this too far. Otherwise sensible parents actually believe that you will enjoy playing with their children, reading them the same story over and over, and being hit by them as part of a game. 'Look how well you get on together!' they will crow, 'You know you're such a favourite with little Billy.' For this reason I don't suggest you go beyond basic politeness in praising and helping with little Billy, unless you really love Billy, or the fond parents will be convinced that they are doing you a favour by letting you spend so much time with him. Completely sane people start to think like that when they have children, and you shouldn't encourage them.

When Children Visit You

What makes this difficult is also your saving point. Your house is almost certainly not child-proof, and may even be full of dangers for small children. For this reason, you can say all the time, 'I'll just lift him down from there. I don't mind about my ornaments, but I'd hate him to hurt himself.' It is a good idea to try to clear breakables and valuables from the lower part of your living-room before they arrive. This isn't always possible so you must try to make it clear where the danger areas (your computer perhaps) are. Good parents will bring toys for their child to play with, but you might have a quick look round to see if there's anything safe and unbreakable you can give to the child if there's an amusement crisis – empty storage tins and baking tins are a noisy but satisfactory possibility.

If you offer refreshments to children you might be surprised to find that parents nowadays tend not to say, 'Only one biscuit,

Fig. 10. Children can break valuables by mistake.

and you can't have anything else until you've finished the bread and butter anyway.' Don't put out on a plate more than you are willing to have smeared all over your rug is the rule here. And don't think you'll get away with better rations and portions for adults. No parents go for that nowadays: they all insist on sharing everything with their children. Unless you're quite happy with this, I would keep the refreshments to a minimum. It is perfectly reasonable to think that you don't want your food wasted or eaten mostly by a two year old.

For a longer stay, you will have to set down house rules. Ask the parents what their children eat, what sort of food they will require. For tiny children, the parents will probably bring their own food. You also must be able to tell the children off to some extent or at least to say very firmly that they can't do something. Most parents will accept this within reason, and may even be waiting for you to say it.

Bringing up children is exhausting and difficult, and visiting is even more so. Have some sympathy for your poor friends and give them opportunities to rest, to get away from people, to have some privacy. Try to make it clear that you like to have them there, even if there are problems. And let them live in their own time cycles: if the children are very hungry, then find them something even if the meal isn't ready. Allow your adult friends the run of the kitchen to heat up the baby food or keep the children quiet. You'll all be grateful if the children's slide into hunger and bad behaviour is halted. You may think, 'But I just don't know what children eat,' and give up, but you could try to have some basic supplies: milk, bread, yogurt, fruit, cheese – most parents can feed a child on that lot.

Many childless people are surprised and even shocked by the extent to which modern parents seem to allow children their own way: the children eat what they want and wear what they want from a very early age. But (1) this is none of your business (except when it impinges on you, and I will admit that there is nothing more irritating than a child guest who says it doesn't want what's on offer and adds in a whining voice, 'Don't you have any prawns? I like prawns') and (2) don't you spend the rest of the time, when not complaining about this, moaning about how repressive your own parents were in this respect? Don't you hate to remember how you were forced to eat what you didn't like? Well then, have some sympathy for people who are trying to do it differently.

Addressed to Parents

When Childless Friends Visit
They've probably come to see you, you know. They'll want to see the children and get to know them a little, but they almost certainly prefer adult company. Spending time all together is fine, and, if they offer to babysit or mind the children, then by all means accept, but don't leave them alone with the children for hours unless you're sure that's what they want.

Mothers spend half their time complaining they have no-one to have a sensible conversation with, and the other half telling their childless friends about what nursery schools they're thinking about for the twins.

Visiting Childless Friends
Please take toys to entertain the children, and anything that is really vital to their comfort or well-being. You can't expect

childless people to know that you don't give your baby skimmed milk and that your five year old has to have fresh juice. It may also not occur to them that your child is not very flexible about mealtimes and eats earlier than most adults – explain the situation and offer to cook for your child yourself.

Lots of parents like, as far as possible, to treat their children almost as if they were little adults, with the same rights. But you can't expect other people to act like this until the children also take on adult responsibilities.

You might think you could pick up and admire whatever you like in your friend's house, but if you have this right it is mostly because you are unlikely to break it and, if you do, you will be willing and able to pay for a replacement. This is not true for a child and you shouldn't blame your friends if they don't like the child poking into everything in sight.

Food and Drink
You may well feel that your children should have whatever they want, and that's fine in your own house if that's how you're bringing them up, but again you should think twice elsewhere. If an adult guest ate a whole packet of biscuits, or took and half-ate three or four cakes, wouldn't you be horrified as a hostess? Yet parents smile as their children do these things. You should teach them that they cannot treat other people's houses as their own: they should ask before doing things, just as you probably would. If you're staying, you would establish a few ground rules but you wouldn't (I hope) walk past your hostess, without a word, to help yourself to food and drink from the kitchen, and so you shouldn't let your children do that.

Your children may have very hard-to-please tastes, but you shouldn't let your friends discover that from their whining complaints when offered food they don't like. Adults, on the whole, can behave graciously when given food they can't eat. They can accept and pretend to eat it and stock up on bread or salad. Children, until they can be this polite, must learn not to complain and whine to their hostess. If in trouble, a quiet word to their mother and father is what's needed, not loud demands for something else. They are never going to be popular guests (with anyone, ever, anywhere) until they learn this.

Adults with very good manners of their own are strangely tolerant of their own children's rudeness – I think it is this that irritates childless friends. They don't want the child spanked into submission, but some recognition by the parent that this behaviour is childlike but undesirable would help a lot.

At Public Events

Parents should try to keep their children under control. Everyone expects some noise and high spirits at children's parties or at the zoo or an amusement park, but at religious ceremonies, adult social events and concerts children should keep quiet. Everyone has sympathy with a bored and fractious child – and a parent trying to cope – but it's not fair to disturb and ruin the event for other adults (who may have paid to attend or may have paid a babysitter to get away from their own kids), and the child should be removed if the noise is continuous.

18

LOVE LIFE

Going on Dates

What's important here is that everyone knows what they're doing. Traditionally, men still ask women out, but women have always had their own options and the ability to ask men to something or other. It is never impolite to ask someone out, provided you are prepared to take no for an answer.

At the beginning of a relationship it is often convenient for both sides to act as though they were just friends, and inviting the other to something as if inviting a same-sex friend out. This is a very handy attitude, as well as being not far off the truth in many cases: people are often wary about having high hopes and will settle for a good night out. (If you don't need the fiction, it's probably because the two of you are clear enough what you want from each other, and don't need etiquette help anyway.)

So, when asking someone out it is almost essential to have some specific suggestion in mind:

'I was thinking of going to the concert at the Town Hall on Saturday, and I wondered if you'd be interested in coming with me?'

'There's a new Thai restaurant opened up near here, do you fancy giving it a try some time?'

If you want to go and are able to do so, then you simply say, 'Yes,' and make the arrangements.

If you can't go but are delighted to have been asked and would love to go to something else, then say so: 'How nice of you to ask me. I'd love to go but I'm busy right then – let's do it another time. Week after next?'

If you don't want ever to go out with this person, you simply say, 'No – I'm afraid I'm busy that night,' or 'all next week,' or

127

'I'm afraid I don't like Thai food,' or 'I'm rather booked up at the moment – let me get back to you on that.'

What's important is that you tactfully get your message over as easily for both of you as you can, so that if you're not interested there's no loss of face. If you are interested, then do try to come up with a *specific* alternative suggestion, to distinguish this from a brush-off: some women (in particular) are strangely reluctant to do so, fearing they may look as though they're chasing a man, and turn down a date but expect the man to realize that they would come out another time. People aren't mind-readers: give them as big a clue as you can manage that you are regretting having to say 'No'. And, on the other hand, a man should realize that even in this day and age a woman who has asked him out can be left feeling very stupid if he refuses, so he should try to embarrass her as little as possible.

What nobody should do in answer to a casual invitation is say, 'No, I've already got a boyfriend.' Remember the fiction that this was a platonic date. You will have other opportunities to drop this into the conversation.

If you invite someone to something more specific, then you need to make the ground rules clear: 'I'd like to take you as my partner to a wedding/the works dance/a ball,' means you're asking her to go out very particularly as a couple with you. This could be a worry for some people, and they might turn you down just for fear of appearing to commit themselves to a relationship they didn't particularly want. Try this one only if you're pretty sure they'll be pleased to be asked, or if the other person is someone you know quite well and you can ask him as a favour. 'It'd be great if you came with me because it'll be much more fun with a partner,' doesn't sound as though you'll be pouncing on him too much or pretending to your relations that he's a long-standing boyfriend. (In fact, it is usually a very bad idea to take a new partner to anything family-oriented because relations have no idea of tact and will make the most dreadful assumptions, followed up with matching questions.)

Of course, the easiest way to get to know someone better, and to see if you have any chance of getting him or her alone, is to make a general invitation. Either make it spontaneous – as you leave the office say, 'I fancy a drink – how about you?' (no offence or embarrassment in saying 'No'), or you invite her to a dinner or drinks party at your house. Then have as long a conversation as you can, find some interest you have in common (cinema, theatre, chess, foreign food) and then say, 'Oh, but we must do that together some night.' However, it is not generally advisable to pretend an interest in something you know nothing about as you will certainly get caught out very quickly. Much better to say, 'I've never tasted Indonesian food but I'd love to try, especially with someone who knows his way round the menu,' or 'What I need is someone to introduce me to German cinema and get rid of my unreasoning prejudice.'

Who Pays?
Really both parties should pay for themselves. Women still don't earn as much as men in general, but most women prefer to be independent when they can be. If you are a woman and much younger or much poorer than your escort, and you're sure it is a real date, then you can allow him to pay for you if you want to. If you're not sure what he, or you, quite thinks of the date, and he asked you out to somewhere of his choosing, then ask him where it is and then say, 'Is that expensive?' or words to that effect. He can then say, 'We can look at the prices as we go in and if you don't like it we'll go somewhere else,' or 'Yes, but don't you worry your head about that as I'm paying,' (or even, 'No, I'm a cheapskate and as I'm paying I'm taking you to a dive'). You may find this embarrassing but not as embarrassing as sorting it out at the end of the evening.

A few years ago, a woman who was paying her whack was expected to hand over the money discreetly to the man so that he could pretend to pay it all. This is not necessary now, and in these days of credit cards it's not always clear who's paying what anyway. Even if it was, it's no-one's business but your own.

At the End of the Evening
Either side is at liberty to ask for or suggest what they'd like to do next. The other side is at liberty to accept or refuse or make an alternative proposal. All such contributions to the discussion are voiced and received gracefully. Of course, no woman is expected to pay for her dinner in kind, and it is most rude for a man to voice the opinion that he expects something in return for his investment. (Women who pay for men's dinners must not expect sexual favours in return either.)

When the couple separates, it is polite for the man to enquire how she is getting home and will she be all right. Unless she is very young (and her parents have insisted), he does not have to escort her home: grown-up young women expect to make their own arrangements. A polite young man would help her find a taxi or wait with her for her bus (on grounds of security rather than sexism). He may well escort her home in some cases: if he picked her up at the beginning of the evening from her own home, if he lives near her, or if it generally suits both of them. If either party has a car, it's polite to offer the other a lift home.

Staying the Night
If you wish to go home together, that is not a question of etiquette, and you are on your own. However, you could just read through the section on staying the night with friends (page 67). A lot of it won't apply to a romantic stay, but you should take particular notice of the section on your hostess's flatmates (page 69). It is polite to inconvenience them as little as possible and to remember that, however much your partner loves you, the flatmate has certain rights and privileges in the flat.

PART THREE
BAD NEWS

19

DEATH

All etiquette should be based on courtesy, kindness and consideration for others, and this is even more true when disasters strike. Etiquette for such times should be thought of as a guide, not a set of strict rules, and should be infinitely flexible.

What's common to all bad news situations is that those most affected have the right to choose their reactions, and their friends should not try to dictate to the afflicted but should match the other's mood. This applies at the most basic level. If someone does not want to discuss his sufferings with you, then you must respect that.

Of course everyone, including the bereaved, should try to observe certain simple bounds of politeness and decency. Mere manners – and this chapter – cannot alleviate grief and unhappiness: all we can do is help set and define those bounds so that bad times are no worse than they need to be.

Old-style etiquette was sometimes based on assumptions that just don't hold true today. People often lived in one place, in one community, all their lives. Everyone knew each other's parents and children. When someone died most of their friends and relations would be nearby: to attend the funeral, to call at the house, to deliver a wreath in person. All the customs are based on this, whereas nowadays by the time they're thirty many people have grown up in one town, gone to college in another, and have lived and worked in a couple more, and all these places may have been hundreds of miles apart.

So the deaths closest to you emotionally may be far from close geographically: a parent's death could mean a long journey for the funeral, and only a very short stay in the family home because you can't take much time off work. It's a shame because you can't spend time with the rest of the family or help sorting through the deceased's belongings, but it's the way life is today. It's also true that if you lived fifty years ago your best friend's mother might be someone you knew very well – if your friend wasn't married he probably lived at home – and when she died it would be a big deal for you too. Nowadays if your best friend's mother dies, she may be someone you've never met, she may have lived too far away for you to attend the funeral and you may feel you're not much support to your friend.

In what follows I've tried to take these factors into account.

Death Close to You

There are well-oiled wheels for organising a funeral and the other formalities of death. The doctor or hospital authorities, a minister of religion, if you belong to a church, and the undertaker will normally help and advise. A good undertaker will handle almost everything, explaining the options at every point.

The other main responsibility of the family (in most of what follows, 'family' can be taken to mean the immediate circle of the deceased, including lovers/partners, step-family, etc.) is to let people know: someone should volunteer to make the phone calls. This will have a knock-on effect. If you tell, for example, an old schoolfriend, he or she may be willing to call all the rest of that group of friends. An announcement in the local newspaper is usual (the undertaker can advise on this too). The announcement should take whatever form the family wants. Some people take a high, sneering line over poems and flowery tributes, but there is no right and wrong in these matters.

Funerals are a dramatic way of marking the end of someone's life. They can also be very expensive. That is fine if the family wants that or there is plenty of money around, but no-one should ever feel obliged to spend too much. What is important here is that the family gets what it wants and is not intimidated into spending more than it can (or, equally, discouraged from having something seen as 'too flashy' or 'common' by advisers). It is the height of bad manners for other mourners to criticize the arrangements, so don't bother worrying about the possibility. Consult only the immediate circle of the deceased. Whom this circle includes must vary and cannot be laid down authoritatively. A generous spirit is needed to avoid hard feelings and family jealousies.

CLICHÉ 1: *'It's what he would have wanted.'*
If you can say this with a clear conscience, use it to the hilt.
Don't hesitate to say, loudly and clearly, 'He often told me he
thought it was a waste of time to have an expensive coffin.'
Cliché 1 is often used to justify outrageously selfish behaviour
('He knew I got upset at funerals, he'd have wanted me to go
ahead with my lunch date instead') so it may as well be used for
good ends as well.

Closely connected is:

CLICHÉ 2: *'He wouldn't have wanted us all to mourn, he'd have
wanted life to carry on.'*
This may have limited use (for example, trying to persuade a
desolate widow to return to normal life, reassuring a friend who
couldn't make the funeral for a good reason) but otherwise . . .
over to An Honest Person: 'When I die, I do want you to mourn,
I want the world to come to a halt, I want everyone to be sad
and cry buckets, and I don't want anyone saying, "She would
have wanted us to carry on." ' I think, secretly, we're most of us
the same.

If people write or send sympathy cards or flowers, it is correct
to write thanks or acknowledgements – which need be only very
brief if you want. However, nobody is likely to criticize you too
much if you really can't face it or if the numbers of tributes
forbid it. You could have an acknowledgement printed or
photocopied for distribution: 'The family of the late Colman
Walsh thank you most sincerely for your kind expression of
sympathy in their recent bereavement.'

When You Are Not the Immediate Family
If a friend, acquaintance or more distant relative dies, you have
three obligations:

1.   Pay your respects to the chief mourner (partner, parent or
      child of the deceased) or to your contact with the family.
          This can take whatever form you feel appropriate: a few
      sentences at the funeral or over the phone. Many people
      hesitate to call a bereaved household, but, if you're sure it's
      the right thing to do, then go ahead, provided you explain
      carefully to whoever answers that you don't want to be a
      trouble, you'll ring off if not convenient or if X doesn't feel
      like talking.

House visits are very common in some circles and communities: local practice and your own sense of what's right should be your guide. As with most matters surrounding a death, you can't tell what's best. It can seem a terrible ordeal for some people – they don't want to talk to friends, however well-meaning. Others are proud and pleased to welcome guests, and see it as a tribute to the dead person. Yet others are just glad to be kept busy talking and making cups of tea. Try to be sensitive to the family's wishes, and above all don't be judgmental and critical of their arrangements.

You may prefer to write to them. A shortish, handwritten letter is the ideal here and is always correct. It really does not need to be long or difficult or formal. Be sympathetic and natural. An example:

Dear John,

I was so sorry to hear of your mother's death. Although I only met her a few times, she was always very welcoming and hospitable to me – I know all your friends felt at home in her house. I can imagine how much you will miss her.

Please pass on my sympathy to your brothers and sisters. I hope to see you soon.

Yours sincerely/With love/With deepest sympathy [whichever you think appropriate]

This isn't a letter-writing era, however, and although some people are rather snooty about sympathy cards they are a reasonable alternative for those who really can't face writing a letter.

Many Roman Catholics send Mass cards for the dead: they pay for a Mass for the soul of the deceased and send a card to the family informing them of this, which solves the problems of paying respects.

2. Go to the funeral or memorial service if this seems appropriate and possible. Don't worry too much if you would like to go and can't because it's too far or you have serious unbreakable commitments. If you think your absence would be noticed, then you should explain briefly but convincingly to the bereaved family by note or phone call.

If you have travelled some distance and perhaps arrive

at the last minute and have to rush off early, don't worry at all – you will find everyone is most understanding and appreciative of the effort you made.

You don't have to be draped in black from head to foot, and in fact this could look rather excessive when the immediate family may not be in full mourning.

Special mourning clothes are not the norm in modern life, but even if some at the funeral are in full black you should not feel embarrassed or under-dressed if you are not. Many people like to wear something dark or sober, and you should dress as respectably as you can, but don't worry about it. Women do not normally have to wear a hat. It is certainly true that nearly all bereaved families are pleased and grateful that you came, not ready to lay into your dress sense or to see disrespect where none was intended.

Afterwards you may be greeted by a member of the family on the way out of the service – it is perfectly fine to say just, 'I'm so sorry,' and move on. Apart from anything else, they've got loads of people to greet. You may be invited to attend the burial or cremation, and to go to some kind of reception afterwards.

These are the minimum requirements. It is not essential to do anything else. This is true of the most closely bereaved too. You do not have to view the body, attend the burial or cremation, or attend any reception unless you want to. Some people do and some people don't, and it is an entirely personal choice.

3. Respect the wishes of the family.

If they say, 'No flowers,' don't send them. (Otherwise it's up to you. There's no obligation, but you might like to if you can't attend the funeral. Any florist will deal with the details for you.) If they say, 'Funeral Private', then leave them to it unless they invite you.

After the Funeral

We can't all hope for the events of the post-funeral party in the splendid Agatha Christie book of this name ('But he was murdered, wasn't he?'), but if you've never been to a reception after a funeral you may be surprised at what jolly events these normally are. Don't skip it because you think it will be depressing – it won't. They are normally a fine opportunity to have a word with the bereaved, to meet up with old friends, and to swap good stories about the deceased. Refreshments can range from a cup of tea and a biscuit to strong drinks and a full meal. (This is not, by the way, technically a wake. A wake is held in the presence of the body, before the funeral, and the point – whatever you've seen in the movies – is meant to be watching the body and saying prayers, not having a wild drunken party.)

CLICHÉ 3: *'She would have wanted to die like that, with her family with her at the end.'*

CLICHÉ 4: *'It was best she went quickly, she wouldn't have wanted to be ill a long time.'*

Yes, they're clichés, trite even, but they are also often true, and there is nothing wrong with everybody batting them round amongst each other.

In the Weeks That Follow
There are three important points:

1. Don't avoid the bereaved. It sounds incredible (*you* would never do this, would you?) but some people cross the street rather than talk to a new widow or a man who's lost his mother. This is awful, dreadful behaviour. Of course the bereaved notice, and how do you think it makes them feel? It is the worst example of people using their own shyness or embarrassment as an excuse for bad behaviour.

2. When you do speak to them, don't avoid the subject. This is slightly tricky, because different people want different things after their loved ones die. But don't pretend it hasn't happened. If nothing else, say, 'How are you feeling now?' to show some concern.

3. Follow the lead of the bereaved. They will, overtly or by implication, indicate how much they want to talk about the death. Don't try either to shut them up or draw them out – let them make the decision.

This brings us to a particularly tricky situation, one that often occurs at college or work. Someone you know reasonably well loses a parent or partner. You didn't know the dead person or only very slightly. Your colleague disappears for a day or two for the funeral, then re-appears. How do you act?

Many people are embarrassed by this. I think it may be that we often have light-hearted friendly relations with others, where everything is treated as a joke. One feels a fool suddenly saying something serious, as if it were pompous or stupid. But it is important to say something. This is a very good simple sentence: 'I was so sorry to hear you had some bad news.' Some variant of this will cover a lot, and it is a line worth remembering. To be brutal, it even works if you can't remember whether it was the mother or father who died. More importantly, it gives your colleague the chance to choose to: (1) mumble his thanks and change the subject; (2) say, 'Yes, I'm very sad that he's gone but he had a good innings. And do you know, there were 250 people at the funeral?'; or (3) 'Bad news? I'm glad to see the back of her.' (That would surprise you, wouldn't it?) As before, allow the bereaved to dictate the pace.

If you'd met or spoken to the dead person or had heard about her a lot, then try to say a few words about her. There is nothing wrong with having them rehearsed and ready for the occasion. Don't be embarrassed: even if normally you converse only in insults, it will be all right. Say, 'She always sounded delightful the way you used to talk about her,' or 'I've never forgotten how nice he was to me when I met him: we had a chat about football and I was so interested in his memories.' You may think it comes out stilted or over-formal but your colleagues will almost certainly be pleased and will repay in kind. You can then go back to calling each other names and conspiring to overthrow the boss. Don't underestimate yourself: people do notice whether or not you say anything, and they do mind, so make the effort. You'll both be glad you did.

With Closer Friends

Keep in touch after the funeral when things may go quiet – the bereaved may want someone to talk to then. But don't treat them as invalids or mental cases, just act as you would have before.

Give them the chance to talk about the dead person if they want. They may not want to, but . . . listen to someone who works as a local reporter: 'I often have dealings with bereaved families. If you're muttering about "tabloid journalism" and "intrusion into private grief", then kindly stop. Most of the families expressly invited me into their houses and their lives and they were glad to co-operate in publicising their son's or wife's story, for various reasons – pride if their child had died a hero, a sad hope of bringing the guilty to justice if there was a crime.

'Long after their child or wife had been buried – and the story slipped from the news – relations would phone me up to talk to me. One mother specifically said to me, "You are the only person who actually listens to me talking about Stephen. Everyone else tries to stop me talking about him. They're all bored by now, they want to get on with other things." I'm sure there is something to be said for encouraging people not to dwell on their griefs, but I was constantly surprised by the extent to which the bereaved wanted to talk and claimed there was no-one to listen.'

So give as much of your time as you can to listening.

It can be difficult to know what to do about those who've lost a partner. You may wish to invite them to social events – where they would previously have attended as a couple – but be unsure they'll want to attend. I think the important thing is to invite them, as soon after the funeral as possible, but be ready for a refusal. Ask them tactfully, stressing that you're not sure if they'll feel like it but they'd be welcome. Be prepared for any response. Don't invite someone to make up the numbers with them unless quite a lot of time has passed and you're sure that's what they'd like.

Most people would much rather you talked about their dead friends in a normal tone of voice, remembering them as they were and neither avoiding the subject nor pretending they were saints.

Terminal Illness

Most of us will admit to a problem with dealing with this. It's impossible to lay down set rules, but there are some guidelines. First of all, you must allow the person who is ill to dictate the atmosphere. If he wants to be sad, or cheerful, or even (in your view) unnaturally callous or embarrassingly affectionate, then you must allow him that privilege. Don't try to persuade him to act differently. You must respect his wishes: he is surely entitled to decide for himself how to spend his last days.

Secondly, you must not thoughtlessly allow your own feelings to interfere with your consideration for him. It may well be hard to visit him, hard to think of anything to say, hard to keep going, but to decide not to visit a dying person often, 'Because it upsets me and so probably isn't good for him either,' is the height of selfishness and bad manners.

Last Word

'Embarrassment' is a word which, with its variants, crops up a lot in this section. Death is a situation we don't often have to cope with, so we're not sure what to do, so it's not surprising we get embarrassed. Try to remember that goodwill and kindness of heart can smooth over the difficult bits. And one other piece of advice (probably true throughout life but particularly true around death): you have something you feel you 'ought' to say, but it's going to be difficult and – that word again – embarrassing. Think: is it difficult because it's a criticism or likely to cause a row? Then shut up. Is it difficult because it's more sentimental or emotional than your normal conversation? Then make the effort and say it.

20

DIVORCE

Everyone knows that divorce is a way of life and is becoming increasingly common. But we all also know that it is not good news and is hard on everyone concerned. There are stories of couples who split and coped, who still like each other, who greet each other with glad cries of delight. But then we think, 'If they liked each other that much why did they split up?' and it's the oddness of such couples that gets the anecdotes repeated.

If it is you who is getting divorced, then etiquette has little to do with your situation. Good manners can help to keep the matter civilized: be kind and courteous, try not to involve the children. But we all know this is going to be hard to stick to. Emotions take over and manners fly out of the window. And I know, I just know what you're going to say: 'Well I tried to be reasonable and polite, but he/she behaved like a monster.' All I can advise is that you try to maintain the basic civilities – even if your opposite number doesn't – and you will be glad afterwards. The emotional perils and battlefields are beyond the scope of this book, and there is little advice on etiquette I can give you directly, but it may help if you read through the section for the friends and relations of divorcers and have a small stock of vague remarks ready to turn away questions:

CLICHÉS 1-4: *'It wasn't working out/I want to make a fresh start/It's just one of those things/Best that we find out now rather than later.'*

Now to the friends of a divorcing couple. (The legal elements may differ but for most of this the term can be taken to cover any couple who are parting.)

With close friends you may hear of the break-up through a distraught phone call, or even from a sobbing figure on the doorstep. Etiquette is not needed: you know what to do when a friend is in trouble and you also know how seriously to take it all. Some couples thrive on three break-ups and reconciliations a year and there's no use outsiders getting too worried.

But when a friend tells you in a social situation that she and Bob are parting, you need to exercise tact and care. You can treat it as a specific form of social announcement and say, 'I'm very sorry to hear that. You'd been together quite a while, hadn't you?'

She may wish simply to inform you of something she feels you would want to know (rather as if she had changed jobs or moved house) or she may want to tell you all the details. It is up to you to give her the chance to react how she wants, and up to her to dictate the level of revelation in the conversation.

If someone wants to tell you really intimate details which you'd rather not hear, then you're in a tricky situation. Say, 'I hope you won't regret telling me this,' with a semi-joking smile. It's rude and, more to the point, almost impossible to shut someone up who's trying to tell you details of a disaster.

The one piece of advice that everyone gives and which really is a golden rule is, 'Don't agree too vehemently when someone tells you his partner is a louse. Don't say, "I said all along he was no good." ' These are always the ones who go back to the louse the next day, then the two of them can't forget what you said and ill wish you for the rest of your life. Best friends have special privileges here, but even for them it's a mistake to agree too vehemently with another's criticism of her lover.

Matters are bad enough when your primary friendship is with one partner. If you know and like both, then you could be in real trouble.

You may well have to choose to some degree. You probably can't be equally friendly with both, at least to begin with, if only because of the possibility of them turning up on your doorstep to cry on your shoulder at the same time. You just have to play it by ear. In this case it is always worth trying occasionally to put in a word for the absent party: 'Come on though, it's nonsense to say you were never happy with him,' or 'I know you're miserable, but I don't expect she's too happy right now either.'

However, that is as far as you should go. The first rule is: don't get involved, other than as a listener. Don't act as go-between. Don't try to arrange a reconciliation. You might think in your naivety that it's your role as a good friend to try to help. You may have a fond picture of yourself as the saviour of the marriage, but it's useless and dangerous to interfere in other people's relationships.

The fascinating thing about divorce is that all divorced people complain they were cheated on the divorce settlement. Of course, divorce is a black hole for money: lawyers are expensive, and dividing things in two (belongings, houses, salaries) is not going to be either easy or profitable. A solicitor says, 'There simply isn't enough money to go around. And with property prices so high, the situation is going to get worse if anything. Women with children do seem to get the worst of the deal though, and that won't change as long as women are seen as the primary carers of children and don't earn as much as men.' It's probably a ludicrously idealistic feminist dream, but it would be nice if second wives bucked the stereotype, stopped criticizing and hating their predecessors, and tried to ensure first wives were treated fairly. If only for selfish reasons – Worldly-Wise Aunts say, 'If he left No. 1, he might leave you. If No. 1 left him, then what's wrong with him? And if he treats her badly in the divorce, how do you think that bodes for you in a few years' time with two small kids?'

But second wives usually have no sympathy or generosity for their predecessors. One divorced wife wanted more maintenance for herself and her two toddlers. The second wife, in all serious-ness, offered to employ No. 1 to clean her house – 'That'll bring her in more money. I'd pay her the going rate.'

If you are still friendly with both parties to a divorce, then you should consider the implications for your social life, but don't let them run it. You probably shouldn't invite them to a small dinner party together unless you're sure they'd be pleased. For a larger function, it would depend on the circumstances. You might like to let each know the other will be there, but if one of them doesn't like it, or tries to present an ultimatum, then he or she must be the one who doesn't come. Divorced people have no business trying to ruin everyone else's lives too.

Parents
It can be a tremendous shock for even the most adult, grown-up person to find out that his parents' marriage is breaking up, and all concerned should try to have some consideration for the others.

In nearly all cases, neither parent is wholly to blame or wholly bad, and the children are usually reluctant to take sides. (I shall use 'child' and 'children' to refer even to adult offspring in what follows.) This is much the best attitude, and you should resist any attempt to turn you against the other parent.

Even if you are an adult, you are an interested party in this divorce and you should try to insist that both parents talk to you and tell you what's going on. You should also feel able to tell them what you think (politely, of course).

But you have responsibilities too: it is your right not to take sides or act as go-between or stir things up, but it is also your duty. You should try to listen to your parents, but tread warily: children feel they know their parents' marriage and characters very well, but you may be in for some surprises. Treat them as normal human beings. If your mother falls in love with someone new, it is hard to talk to her as you would a friend in a similar situation, but you should try. You must draw a line between involvement (they're your parents) and interference (they have their own lives to lead).

Even if your parents have been parted for some time, it can be hard to accept their finding new opposite-sex friends. This is natural but also unreasonable. You must try to persuade yourself to behave – even if you don't much feel like it.

First of all, try to separate your reluctance to grant your parents a love life from your feelings about the person concerned. Say your mother finds a new man. He is probably quite reasonable (your mother chose him after all), it may be just the idea you object to. This can be on several grounds: you still hope she might get back with your father, you feel pushed out by the new relationship, you don't like the thought of your mother with a lover, you don't think he's right for her.

But you have to remember that you have your own life to lead and she has hers. You may be living at home or nearby now, but soon you may move away, lead your own life, even marry. You won't want to be the centre of your parents' lives then; you might even be glad that she has a lover.

And, in the end, it isn't for you to say what your mother does. It just isn't your business. Assuming you're adult, how do you feel if she tries to dictate in your life? Even if you think the new lover is awful, then (I'll say it again) you shouldn't interfere in other people's relationships because you don't know enough about them. Give your poor mother a break.

You may feel that a lot is being asked of you, and it is, but it will be worth it if you manage to keep in contact and on reasonable terms with both parents.

Step-parents

This is such a thorny and individual area that it is hard to bring etiquette into it. But, roughly speaking, if you hate your step-parent you still have the same obligations as you would have if one of your friends married someone you didn't like. That is, you have to behave with normal civility to the hated spouse and you have to see him or her occasionally. You can arrange to see only your natural parent most of the time, but there will be occasions when you must invite or meet your step, and then you must be polite. You can expect the same behaviour towards you. (If antagonistic steps have to live in the same house, this is not going to be enough but it is also, I'm glad to say, outside the scope of this book.)

Second weddings: you may not want to watch your father re-marry but you ought to go if he wants you there. On the other hand, he ought not to insist that you are, say, a bridesmaid if you don't want to be.

If you get married, you must invite your step-parent as well as your natural parents. (As before: if your friend was married to someone you didn't like, you'd still invite them both, wouldn't you?)

This is to take a worst case view, of course. Most people at least negotiate a truce with a step-family, and lots develop a very good relationship. A step-parent can be a useful friendly adult, well-intentioned towards you and sympathetic, but not as easily shocked and worried as a natural parent. He or she can also act as a good sounding-board or intermediary when asking something difficult of a natural parent. If you can reach an understanding, then you can often find a good friend.

21

UNEMPLOYMENT AND MONEY TROUBLES

If You are Unemployed
You need tell other people only as much as you want to. It's perfectly reasonable to say, if asked what you do, that you're between jobs or looking for work, but there's also no reason to be ashamed of being unemployed.

If You are not Unemployed
What do you say when someone tells you he's lost his job?

That you're sorry. That you hope he'll get something else soon. That you hope he's not in too severe financial straits. He probably is, but there's not a lot you can do except seem sympathetic. On the other hand, don't overdo it. Unemployment for most people isn't the end of the world and isn't permanent, so acting as if it was a terminal illness, or the worst thing you could ever imagine happening to anyone, isn't helpful. Your friend may be trying to keep his spirits up and look on the bright side so don't go too mad on the, 'Oh how dreadful, poor you,' line. Better to act as if it's obviously only a temporary situation.

Unwanted advice can be annoying, and so can remarks like, 'Still no job? What are you going to do now?'

There is a tendency to say, when someone tells you he's lost his job and is looking for another, 'Oh I know someone who works in that field/owns a company/might be looking for someone.' We do it with a vague idea of being helpful, of trying to cheer up the jobless one. But I think you should keep quiet, unless you really think you can help, and intend to try. If you're not sure, then say nothing. You can always contact your lead first to see if there really is any hope in that direction. But you might be surprised how much a casual remark from you is seen as a potential life-saver to the unemployed. You've forgotten it (and done nothing) but your friend is busily telling other people, 'Old X thought he might know of something I could try for, I'm still waiting for him to get back to me on it.' It may not be important to you, but it's important to him.

People who live in depressed areas quickly learn to replace the question, 'And what do you do?' in social life with, 'Do you work?' and the rest of us might well try that out too. It's already much in use for mothers with small children, who universally reply, 'Yes, but I don't get paid for it. I work looking after my children.' The jobless, too, often give smart replies. ('I'm a writer – I sign my name every week,' or 'I'm a government artist – I draw the dole.') Be patient with them, it's boring having to tell people the whole time you're unemployed.

An Unemployed Person says, 'I couldn't say I was the victim of much prejudice or bad manners. One thing – and I don't blame people for this – is that those with money don't understand a situation in which 50 pence can be important. And they shouldn't assume that just because you're on the dole you've got nothing to do all day. I order my time as well as I can, but some people assume that I'm always free to talk to them or help them out, or that I couldn't possibly have any plans that can't be instantly dropped or put off. I'd like to advise people not to be embarrassed when they say, "Don't you pay for a round, we know you're broke," but as nobody ever does say this I don't need to.' Despite this, care and tact should be exercised in trying to help out or subsidize the jobless (or otherwise poor). Don't be patronizing. If someone arranges to go out for the evening, he will have planned to pay for himself. If an unexpected expense arises during the course of a social event (a taxi ride, or meal out), then that might be the moment for an offer of help or a loan.

Money Troubles
Often (but not always) connected with unemployment. If you're falling into debt or worried about money, you can get plenty of advice, e.g. from a Citizens' Advice Bureau. Dealing with your debts isn't exactly a matter of etiquette, except where it touches your social life. You may like to give a few close friends an inkling that things are going wrong. You can then bravely say, 'I

can't join in,' when expensive outings are proposed, or suggest cheaper alternatives, or arrange to join a group of theatre-goers for a drink before or after. Nobody should think twice about such things: especially as most people have money problems at some time in their lives.

If you are temporarily poor, then you should try not to take offence if friends try to help. It's human nature to get touchy and proud but try to be logical – 'He insisted on paying for my meal in a restaurant, and I wish he hadn't. He said I'd helped him out, he was returning the favour, but I was embarrassed. Well, yes, I *had* helped him out – I had time to spare because of having no job – but still . . .' It's only reasonable to do favours for favours, and a time favour is the equal of a money favour. Whatever the circumstances, I can only encourage you to try to be gracious if someone has embarrassed you or hurt your pride in a well-meaning way.

Of course, those not facing money troubles should be tactful too. If you want to go somewhere, and your friends say, 'No, I can't afford it,' then the answer is not necessarily to say, 'I'll pay for us all.' Your friends may feel they can't accept this offer, but can no longer refuse to go. You've just forced them into expenditure they don't want. And you can never be sure how important that money is to them: they may not be mean just because they don't seem poor and haven't told you their troubles.

Presents – the Awful Truth
If you have no money you may be worried about Christmas or about not being able to give presents at other times. But the thought *does* count. The rather sentimental truth is that people will be knocked-out and grateful if you give them something that you made yourself, or something small and cheap and amusing or well-chosen (jokes or toys from a children's shop, a gadget to re-seal a wine bottle). Don't compare the presents you give with those you receive, whether you're rich or poor. It's unnecessary and irrelevant.

PART FOUR
COMMUNICATIONS
AND CLASS

22

NAMES

The traditional etiquette questions: forks in restaurants, mixing with the upper classes and fearing your lack of breeding will show, not knowing how to introduce a Brigadier General to a female Vice-Chancellor – all these I can cut through with my knife of good sense, goodwill and flexibility. You'll have noticed I've been busy telling you that no-one is likely to mind, it doesn't really matter if you get it slightly wrong, there is no right or wrong. No-one will notice or take offence, I say blithely, it will all be all right.

Unfortunately, we are entering a positive minefield where, sadly, this is no longer true. People who would behave with supreme tact and tolerance – and with perfect etiquette – if you broke a vase in their house are likely to get terribly offended if you addressed them as Miss instead of Ms, or Mr instead of Dr. You, who meant no harm and couldn't possibly have known, are probably bearing the brunt for all those other people who didn't bother to get it right when they should have and could have, or who are sexist or make unwarranted presumptions. In what follows I can tell you what I think is the sensible modern way to address people or to find out how to address them, but I feel obliged to keep warning you that you still may be criticized in these areas: there are no universal answers.

We often have to work out a way to address people before we have enough information on what they would prefer. If you are corrected very coldly, then you must say, 'I'm sorry if I got it wrong: tell me exactly your name.' But bear with these people, and remember that everybody does have a right to decide for themselves what their name and designation is. You should not argue or question it. This is not the Eurovision Song Contest,

153

you do not get a vote. It is entirely correct and sensible for someone to put you right about his name as politely as possible. If he is not as polite as you like, this may be to try to forestall criticism. (Any woman who keeps her own name after marriage finds that the whole world feels entitled to comment on and very likely to criticize this decision, so we can get a little defensive. See also separate section on addressing women, below.)

If you have to phone or meet someone when you only know their names and not their designation, then you have to take a chance. There are two problems here: ambiguous names, e.g. Jocelyn, and designations for women. (A third problem is that someone may have a title – Dr, or the Honourable, or whatever – but then it is up to him to tell you as you can't possibly be expected to know that.)

Ambiguous Names
When writing, ringing up or arriving at a reception desk, you give the name in full: 'Jocelyn Smith.' Full name on an envelope is fine with no designation (whatever your secretarial college told you) but I must warn you that writing 'Dear Jocelyn Smith' is seen as the most dreadful error in some circles. This is a pity, as it is a useful formulation for exactly these circumstances, but there you go. I think it must be politer than giving someone the wrong gender. However, you should bear in mind that Jocelyn may be mighty tired of surprising people, but, on the other hand, he or she is also used to it, and won't fall off the chair with surprise. You may also come across this problem with a fore-name from an unfamiliar culture.

Women
Ms, Miss or Mrs? This is a fraught one indeed. It seems to me that Ms is the obvious solution for addressing women one doesn't know: polite, easy and quick to spell and write, and who are all these people who can't pronounce it? If they can say Miz, then they've said Ms. Miz has been in use in southern parts of the USA for a long time, and, before Ms had feminist connotations, businesses were already putting M/s on envelopes to unknown women, apparently without family life as we know it coming to an end.

Ms is a particularly useful title for married women who use their maiden name either professionally or all the time – Mary Jones, married to John Smith, cannot correctly be described as either Miss or Mrs Jones. It was time for an easy compromise, and Ms fills that role admirably.

However, there are women who hate to be addressed as Ms, and these are often the same ones who hate to be addressed as Miss if they're Mrs and vice versa. It is up to them to give their preferred designation when they introduce themselves or sign letters.

Getting it Right

You should try to remember people's preferences: once you've been given the name and designation it is very bad manners to get it wrong. In all business situations it is entirely correct to phone up someone's organization and ask for her correct name and title or, 'How should I address a letter to . . .' (just as you might ask for the name of their sales director or human resources officer). You may ask either the switchboard operator or the person's secretary. You probably won't be asked who you are but there's no reason not to say: it's nothing to be ashamed of.

First Names

A lot of people assume that this is an era of great informality and the use of first names must be universal amongst all adults. They are very severely mistaken. For a start, not everyone grew up recently, or subscribes to the alleged values of the current era. But even young people well used to informality in many areas of life can find themselves put out when someone they don't know, who is trying to sell them something, uses their first name. This is such bad business practice that it is hard to believe that anyone does it, but they do. Even more maddening is for strangers to address a Stephen as Steve or an Elizabeth as Liz. Don't do it.

Roughly speaking, you shouldn't assume you can use the first name of anyone who is senior to you at work, or older than you, or whom you have never met before. It is never wrong *not* to use first names, but it may sound over-formal, and, if someone uses your first name, then you will undoubtedly sound repressive or unfriendly or as if you are administering a put-down if you don't reciprocate.

It is always for an older (or more senior) person to invite a younger to use a first name. Some young people assume older people like to be treated as younger, and that this means using first names, but they're probably wrong, and it's never wise to assume. Of course, lots of old people are friendly and may like modern informality, but you should leave it to them to suggest it. They were probably brought up never to use first names except with close friends of the same age, and it may come very oddly to them to hear you being so matey. In fact, the general effect may not be matey at all, but rude or cheeky or undignified. Bear in mind that everyone has a right to choose his or her own name and designation.

In general, as I say, being formal is never wrong. But you should watch for one situation, particularly found amongst women. A woman not much older than you might be offended if you call her Mrs Brown, on the grounds that you appear to be stressing her age and implying you are much younger, or part of a much younger circle who use first names. She may resent this, so be careful.

Divorcees

If a woman who took her husband's name is now divorced, then the only way to find out what to call her is to ask her. In this day and age it would be foolish to lay down strict rules or say what's right or wrong. Some women decide after a first marriage that they're tired of changing their name and they'll stick with their husband's name: thus it can happen that a woman re-marries but keeps her first husband's name.

Women at Work

In business a woman may call herself what she wants, but she'd better not try to call herself Mrs John Smith (unless, perhaps, she's the Vice-President of John Smith Industries). It simply isn't professional. And Mrs Sheila Smith sounds wrong to many people. Ms Sheila Smith seems the ideal solution yet again.

Widows

A widow is correctly addressed by her married name as if her husband was still alive: Mrs John Smith. If she doesn't want you to call her that, then she will tell you and you must respect her wishes. There may be a generation difference here: a woman widowed in her sixties may like to keep her husband's name for the rest of her life, where a young widow may see things differently. It is also true that if you never knew the dead husband you may feel odd writing to her in his name (you may

well not even know it) and you are free to call her Mrs May
Noble. She may put you right, but she probably won't be
offended.

Titles of All Kinds

At the end of this chapter you will find a table of formal titles. If
you are about to write to or meet a titled public personage and
are still not sure, then you can always phone up his or her office
and ask what the correct form is – the staff will be used to such
questions.

If you come across titles in your social life, there are a few
things to remember.

A man's title generally spreads in some way to encompass his
wife: Lord and Lady, the Hon Mr and Mrs, Sir John and Lady
(she may be Lady John or Lady Mary or Lady Reed).

If a woman has a title, it does not roll on to her husband: she
may be a Dame, or she may have inherited a title through her
father. If she inherits an Hon, then she keeps that even if she
changes her name on marriage: Mr and the Hon Mrs Jones. If
she is a Lady in her own right – daughter of an Earl, Marquess
or Duke – and marries a non-titled gent, then they are Mr John
and Lady Serena Chambers.

There is a certain logic to it all, but getting it right depends on
knowing the exact status of your friends: Knight? Baronet?
Peer? If you don't know how exactly they got their title, then you
may get it wrong, so just ask. If friends your own age have titles,
they shouldn't, I think, expect you to use them except – just
about – on formal (wedding) invitations and *maybe* on envelopes
of Christmas cards.

Professional Titles

Many doctors, whether academic or medical, don't use their
titles outside work: and in a purely social situation it is not
necessary to introduce a doctor with his title, unless he makes it
clear this is what he wants.

Members of the clergy do keep their titles at all times. That's
not to say you can't use their Christian names if invited, just that
they should normally be introduced with their title. The main
Church of England titles are listed at the end of the chapter.
When faced with another faith, or one different from your own,
you simply ask; the clergyman will tell you what he's comfortable
with.

Addressing Royalty

You do not normally address the Queen or the more senior members of the Royal Family first.

On being presented, you use their official verbal address the first time it arises, then move to Sir or Ma'am for the rest of the conversation, as follows:

You address:

The Queen as 'Your Majesty' (first time) then 'Ma'am';

The Duke of Edinburgh as 'Your Royal Highness' then 'Sir';

The Prince of Wales as 'Your Royal Highness' then 'Sir';

Royal Princes and Dukes as 'Your Royal Highness' then 'Sir';

Royal Princesses and Duchesses as 'Your Royal Highness' then 'Ma'am'.

Letters should not be sent directly to the Queen and other members of the Royal Family unless you know them, but should be addressed to the Private Secretary of the personage concerned.

Formal Social Address

The Peerage

On an Envelope:	To Begin a Letter:	Introduced as:	Addressed as:
The Duke of Hyde	Dear Duke of Hyde or Dear Duke	The Duke of Hyde	Your Grace or Duke
The Duchess of Hyde	Dear Duchess of Hyde or Dear Duchess	The Duchess of Hyde	Your Grace or Duchess
The Marquess of Kean	Dear Lord Kean	Lord Kean	Lord Kean
The Marchioness of Kean	Dear Lady Kean	Lady Kean	Lady Kean
The Earl of Main	Dear Lord Main	Lord Main	Lord Main
The Countess of Main	Dear Lady Main	Lady Main	Lady Main
The Viscount Send	Dear Lord Send	Lord Send	Lord Send
The Viscountess Send	Dear Lady Send	Lady Send	Lady Send
Baron and his wife:			
The Lord Denby	Dear Lord Denby	Lord Denby	Lord Denby
The Lady Denby	Dear Lady Denby	Lady Denby	Lady Denby
Baronet and his wife:			
Sir John Dove Bt	Dear Sir John	Sir John Dove	Sir John
Lady Dove	Dear Lady Dove	Lady Dove	Lady Dove
Life Peer and his wife:			
The Lord Bain	Dear Lord Bain	Lord Bain	Lord Bain
The Lady Bain	Dear Lady Bain	Lady Bain	Lady Bain
Knight and his wife:			
Sir Richard McMahon	Dear Sir Richard	Sir Richard McMahon	Sir Richard
Lady McMahon	Dear Lady McMahon	Lady McMahon	Lady McMahon

Church of England Clergy

	ON AN ENVELOPE:	TO BEGIN A LETTER:	INTRODUCED AS:	ADDRESSED AS:
	The Most Reverend and Rt Hon The Archbishop of Canterbury/York	My Lord Archbishop	The Archbishop of Canterbury/York	Your Grace
Other archbishops:	The Most Revd the Lord Archbishop of Blank	Dear Lord Archbishop or Dear Archbishop	The Archbishop of Blank	Archbishop
Bishop of London:	The Rt Rev and Rt Hon the Lord Bishop of London	Dear Bishop	The Bishop of London	Bishop
Other Bishops:	The Rt Rev the Lord Bishop of Blank	Dear Bishop	The Bishop of Blank	Bishop
Deans:	The Very Reverend, the Dean of Dunning	Dear Dean or Dear Mr Dean	The Dean of Dunning	Dean
Vicars and Rectors:	The Reverend John Smith	Dear Mr Smith or Dear Father Smith (whichever he prefers)	Mr Smith or Fr Smith	Mr Smith, Fr Smith, Vicar or Rector

Other

	ON AN ENVELOPE:	TO BEGIN A LETTER:	INTRODUCED AS:	ADDRESSED AS:
High Court Judge:	The Hon Mr Justice Dunn	Dear Judge	Mr Justice Dunn or Sir John Dunn	Sir John
Circuit Court Judge:	His Honour Judge Birt	Dear Sir	Judge Birt	Judge Birt
MP:	Mr John Silver MP or John Silver Esq MP	Dear Mr Silver	Mr John Silver	Mr Silver
Privy Councillor:	The Rt Hon James Jones	Dear Mr Jones	Mr James Jones	Mr Jones
Lord Mayors:	The Rt Hon the Lord Mayor of London/York/ Belfast/Cardiff	Dear Lord Mayor	The Lord Mayor of (city name)	My Lord Mayor
Other Lord Mayors:	The Right Worshipful the Mayor of Blank	Dear Lord Mayor	The Lord Mayor of Blank	My Lord Mayor
Mayor of a city:	The Right Worshipful the Mayor of (city name)	Dear Mr Mayor or Dear Madam Mayor	The Mayor of (city name)	Mr Mayor or Madam Mayor

On an Envelope:	To Begin a Letter:	Introduced As:	Addressed As:
Mayor of a town: The Worshipful Mayor of (town name)	Dear Mr Mayor or Dear Madam Mayor	The Mayor of (town name)	Mr Mayor or Madam Mayor
Medical doctor: Dr James Brown MD	Dear Dr Brown	Dr or Mr Brown (as he prefers)	Dr or Mr Brown
Surgeon (Fellow of Royal College of Surgeons): Mr Simon Smith FRCS	Dear Mr Smith	Mr Smith	Mr Smith

23

ADDRESSING ENVELOPES AND WRITING LETTERS

Business

There are two separate issues here: business and social. In business you must find the correct name and designation of anyone you are writing to if at all possible, and the easy way is to ring up and check. You can use either full forename or initials, and you should add their position in the company:

Ms Jane Brown, Personnel Director

Mr I P Smith, Editor.

If you are writing to a member of the public in a business capacity, then the only sensible designation for an unknown female is Ms, if she hasn't told you her preferred title in her own letter or form. If the name seems ambiguous, then it's easiest to write the name in full with no title.

Socially

Addressing cards or invitations to couples seems to cause untold trouble. If the couple are friends and you write to them often, then you really ought to ask them some time how they like to be addressed. They will know the answer, they will tell you, and then you must write it down in your address book so you can get it right in future. If you are addressing the Christmas cards *now* and can't wait, then read these guidelines.

If the Couple are Married

If you know the woman has changed her name to the man's, then you address them as Mr and Mrs followed by the man's name: Mr and Mrs Nigel Prince or Mr and Mrs N D Prince.

If she hasn't, then you write out their two names separately, in either order, and using Ms (unless you know she hates it).

Mr Nigel Prince and Ms Julia Power

or Mr N Prince and Ms J Power

or no titles:

Julia Power and Nigel Prince

or J Power and N Prince.

If you are not sure about name changes (this is the one you're worried about, isn't it?), then you have two choices: the very informal:

Julia and Nigel

(nothing wrong with this in most circumstances)

or else you have to decide for yourself which you think will insult them more, to be given separate names when they have one or to be treated as Mr and Mrs when they don't call themselves that – both likely responses. If you think you can get away with it (depends on the couple, your relationship with them, and also to some extent on the names), you can call them by both names:

Julia and Robin Slater Speed.

(They may even have changed their names to this which would be helpful.)

But the important thing is to find out so you know for the next time. When your friends get married, you should ask them this question early on. Women may say, 'I'm keeping my own name professionally but taking his in private life,' which means that if you're a friend you use the married name – but in these circumstances it probably won't be that much of a gaffe to call her by her maiden name on an invitation.

If you are addressing a married woman who took her husband's name, then correctly and traditionally you call her Mrs + her husband's name: Mrs John Smith. Fine if you are being formal, or perhaps if she's of a different generation, but it can feel very odd if, say, you're writing a cheery letter to your old schoolfriend whom you think of as Mary Brown. Mrs + her first name + his surname – Mrs Mary Smith – is becoming very common, but this is another of those pitfalls: many people frown on this still, and an older generation will tell you that it sounds as though Mary is divorced. But if you and your friend are happy, then don't worry about tradition.

There is nothing wrong with plain Mary Smith (it is more technically correct than Mrs Mary Smith) and although it is usual to put a designation on an envelope, it is neither rude nor incorrect to put an unadorned name there.

Unmarried Couples
This is another area that seems to bother people. No need. You treat them exactly as described above for married couples who've kept their own names. If you don't know one of their surnames, then you write Nigel and Julia or Nigel Prince and Julia. The second option may give you a moment's qualm but there's nothing actually wrong with it. Just make sure you find out for next time. You could address it solely to the partner you know on the envelope, using both first names on the card or letter inside – most people wouldn't mind that at all.

Letters Generally
It is almost never incorrect to write letters, but phoning and e-mailing are now acceptable in most social situations. To many people, using the phone is second nature, and actually preferable for day-to-day communication. It is quick, immediate and – very important – two-way. An exchange of letters to decide a date for an event might take forever when the matter could have been resolved instantly on the phone or by e-mail.

There are some circumstances in which letters are still prefer-able: letters of condolence when someone dies (see page 136) and proper thank yous for large favours and gifts (any accom-modation that includes overnight stays, wedding presents). Even in these cases I must reluctantly say that a phone call is better than nothing at all. (If you have money but not the time or inclination, sending flowers with a short message is a reasonable replacement for a letter, and the whole operation can be set in motion with one phone call and a credit card.)

Letters have this advantage over phone calls: you choose your time and place to write it, the recipient chooses his time and place to read it – no-one is put out at all. Phone calls have a lot more potential for disruption.

Writing Formal Letters
The rules have eased a lot here, but there are some guidelines to follow:

1. For formal letters always use plain notepaper. (Keep the flowers and Snoopy for letters to friends, not job applications.)

2.   Address, phone number and date in top right-hand corner.

3.   Choose the most appropriate salutation: Dear Mr Smith,
      Dear John (only if you're sure that's not too informal),
      Dear Sir or Madam (when you don't know who the
      recipient will be), Dear Mr or Ms Smith (when answering a
      letter signed S Smith). Dear Jocelyn Jones (slightly
      frowned on but the only easy answer if you don't know
      Jocelyn's designation). Such phrases as Dear Messrs or
      Dear Mesdames (when addressing a partnership of solici-
      tors or dress-shop owners) are not necessary nowadays:
      assume your letter will be read by one person and write
      accordingly.

There are two main layouts for letters:
    Non-indented which means all the lines begin at the left-hand
edge of the page with a line between paragraphs.

Dear Mr Stafford

Thank you for your enquiry of 17 May.

We would be more than happy for you to visit us on the date you
suggest . . .

Indented which means the first line of every paragraph starts
several spaces in from the left-hand margin. A line between
paragraphs is not essential.

    Dear Mrs Perry
        I wrote to you earlier this year about the possibility of
    organizing a fund-raising event.
        It now looks as though we shall be able to go ahead this
    Christmas . . .

Both possibilities are equally correct: what is important is
consistency, that you don't change from indented to non-
indented halfway through. (This also affects the closing.)

4.   There are all sorts of old rules about the closing: you wrote
      'Yours sincerely' if you knew the name of the person you
      were writing to, 'Yours faithfully' if it was Dear Sir. Stick

to that if you wish, though these days most people don't worry. 'Yours truly' or just 'Yours' are other possibilities. Don't think too hard about which most expresses your feelings because they are all very unnatural phrases to be using in a letter to your solicitor. They're just conventions. You then leave a space for your signature and either type or print your full name, with your designation afterwards if you wish. If your letter was indented you centre the lines like this:

Yours sincerely

CHRISTINE LEWRY (Ms)

If non-indented, it looks like this:

Yours sincerely

CHRISTINE LEWRY (Ms)

5.   You write the address as centrally as possible on the envelope.

6.   Don't forget to put the stamp on (top right-hand corner of the envelope, in case you didn't know).

24

THE TELEPHONE

As a Caller

Have clearly in mind whom you want to talk to, and what you are going to say if the person you want does not answer the phone.

You should identify yourself as quickly as possible (and not by saying, 'It's me,' either – nothing is more irritating), checking the number is correct first if you like. What you must not do is cross-question whoever answers, 'What number is that? Who are you? Well, where is she then?' You should be polite anyway, but you have no right to demand information when you are the caller, and particularly not if you have not already explained who you are. Remember, you are calling (usually) uninvited and without warning. This may seem to be putting it strongly if it's a social call, but it is true. The person at the other end may be in the bath, eating a meal or generally inconvenienced by your call. You may well sound more aggressive than you think. Just because you know your intentions are good and friendly does not mean they do, particularly if your first contact is with a flatmate or relative rather than the person you actually want.

Never try funny tricks or fail to identify yourself: particularly if you are a man speaking to a woman. A woman is not only justified but also sensible if she puts the phone down on such a caller. If you are caught out like this, then apologize, don't complain.

If someone goes to fetch the person you want, or offers to take a message, then thank them.

When you get to the person you wish to speak to always enquire first, 'Is this a bad time? Can you talk or should I ring later?' or else, 'Have you got a minute? This won't take long.'

This applies not only to business calls or those to people you want to ask a favour of. You must say it to your best friend or your spouse too.

You may think I'm being hard on callers, but the truth is that most of the population of Britain seems unable to keep in their heads what's necessary for making a successful call. Anyone who takes phone calls from members of the public, or who has placed a classified ad to be answered by phone calls, will confirm this. On the phone people don't say who they are or what they want, they don't have even a first sentence ready, they forget to give some vital fact, they have absolutely no idea of manners, of saying 'please' or 'thank you' or even 'Hello'. All this is time-wasting and irritating.

More Phone Manners
Always try to speak clearly. Don't call someone when you're eating, or with loud music or TV noises in the room. Don't continue your own conversation with someone in the room after the phone has been answered, or keep someone waiting for any other reason. All these things are maddening to the person at the other end (after all, *you* have called and interrupted *them*) and very bad manners.

You never know what you're interrupting when you make a call. Don't indulge in guessing games, and even if you're a long-lost friend sure of your welcome, remember that you may just have called at a time of bereavement, or that your 'favourite couple' may have split up since you last saw them.

Social Hours
Don't make calls at unsocial hours unless (1) it's an emergency or (2) you know the person and their habits very, very well. You should also consider flatmates and relatives: your friend may not mind calls at 1 am or 6 am, but he might not be there and other residents won't appreciate it. For some reason, people think that if they wake someone in the morning with a call, then that's fine, and far from apologizing they'll say, 'Time you were up anyway.' This is the height of bad manners (trying to impose your standards on someone else) and such people deserve to be phoned up at 2 am or whenever they're deepest asleep and told, 'Time you got up and partied.'

Social hours, in the absence of evidence to the contrary, are about 9 am to 10 pm on weekdays, maybe 10.30 am to 10.30 pm at weekends. If you wake someone up, you must apologize, even if you don't think it was an unreasonable time to call. As above, you may defend yourself to the extent of saying, 'I didn't think you'd be asleep,' but not by attacking the other person and their habits. As someone who has worked nightshifts I can tell you that people who accidentally called me when I was asleep during the day might be forgiven, but those who told me off for being asleep never were.

Making Phone Calls Elsewhere

If you use someone else's phone, then you must pay unless the call is very short and local or your friends are very insistent. For long-distance calls you must try to time them and work out the cost realistically. If your friends refuse to take money, then you should limit your calls to the most urgent and keep them short.

Taking Phone Calls Elsewhere

Lots of people think nothing of this, but you shouldn't give others' phone numbers out to all and sundry. It's rude anyway, but they might be ex-directory or have other reasons why they keep it private. In general, don't arrange to be called at someone else's house unless you are a doctor or similar, or the call you're expecting is genuinely urgent. Even so, you must explain the situation to your hostess immediately on arrival, saying that you hope she doesn't mind. If you don't do this, then you can hardly be surprised if some aged aunt who has never heard of you answers the phone and says you're not there. Serves you right.

It is very off-putting when answering the phone in one's own house to hear a peremptory voice demanding to speak to a visitor. If you are trying to track someone down in another's house, then do be extra polite: 'I'm very sorry to disturb you, but I need to contact Audrey Stafford and I understand she's there. Would it be possible to speak to her?'

Answering the Phone

1.   Be polite. The caller may have interrupted you in mid-kiss but he doesn't know that – he hasn't done it deliberately. If you answer the phone in the middle of the night, then you are allowed to be a little bit short, but find out what the caller wants first: it may be a genuine emergency and you'll feel bad if you snapped. On the other hand, if you are not

an early riser, then don't feel embarrassed about telling people, 'I was still in bed actually, you woke me.' If someone regularly calls you too early, then you should ask them not to.

2.   Don't have snappy openers ready or say, 'Whoever you are, you just got me out of the bath,' unless you're prepared to stand by what you say. If you say that and then get upset and worried because you've insulted your mother-in-law or your boss, then you can't expect much sympathy.

3.   Say 'Hello' and give your number or name if you want. You presumably have your own rituals here, and you can choose whatever you want. You have no obligation to give more information than you want to, and if that means just 'Hello?' then that's your business. I'm not suggesting being aggressive about this, but for simple security reasons it is perfectly reasonable to say no more until you know who's calling. If the caller asks for information you're reluctant to give, then you may ask who he is. It is not rude to refuse to give out information on the phone, and you can be as firm as you like about it. You can refuse to talk to people and you can put the phone down and you have committed no breach of manners. If people mess around and won't tell you what you want to know, then it is they who are being rude, not you.

4.   If the call is not for you. In a social situation the world divides sharply into those who don't want you to ask who it is for them and those who do. Both sides find the opposite arrangement very irritating. You must sort this out with the people you live with and find out what they would like you to do, and do it. But if your flatmate says, 'It's for you, I don't know who it is, a man,' you have no right to tell her off for not getting a name unless you pay her and she is your secretary. You can ask people as a favour to screen your calls, but not demand it as a right. Some people feel it is impolite to ask people who they are in this situation, and it is not for you to insist they outrage their feelings.

5.   If your flatmate is in the bath, then I suggest you say, 'He's in the bath at the moment. Is it urgent enough to get him

out or shall I ask him to ring you later?' You shouldn't be asked to conduct remote control conversations through the bathroom door: one urgent question and answer are all that can be expected. If necessary, say firmly, 'I'm afraid I don't have time/can't remember all that and I think it's best if you talk to him yourself later.'

6. Taking a message. Write it down, don't ever assume you'll (a) remember the message and (b) remember to tell it. If you live with others, then a message book attached to the phone is much the best way. Otherwise agree a place for leaving messages. Don't slide bits of paper under doors: they can disappear under the carpet.

7. If you're busy when the call comes. If the other person doesn't ask, then you must just interrupt him and say, 'I'm terribly sorry but I just can't talk to you now,' and give a sketchy reason. (There's no need to go into too much detail: I'm going out/have got visitors, etc. Being in the middle of an ordinary, i.e. no guests, meal is interesting: the caller usually thinks that's not enough reason not to talk, whereas the luncher thinks it is.) Your friend may sound put out, but has no business feeling that way and you shouldn't pay any attention, unless there was a definite arrangement for him to call. One thing though: you must tell him fairly quickly – if you wait until he's gossiped for ten minutes then say, 'I must go as I'm performing open-heart surgery/my boss is sitting waiting for his dinner,' then he'll feel pretty stupid, and he doesn't deserve that.

Unwanted Calls

I am astonished by the number of people who tell me that they don't like to interrupt or end unwanted phone calls. The worst are unsolicited calls from salespeople – the kind who call you at home in the evenings. These people have entered your house uninvited and quite probably at an inconvenient time and you don't have to listen to them, let alone give their call serious consideration. Simply interrupt them the moment they give away who they are and say, 'No thanks, we're not interested,' and put the phone down without even waiting for a reply. This is not rude. If you receive a lot of these unsolicited telemarketing calls you may like to contact the Telephone Preference Service to arrange for such calls to be stopped.

Answering Machines

Leaving a Message

The only essential part of the message is your name: don't say 'It's me' – the machine may distort the voice and can't be questioned. If you want, just say your name: 'Stephen Smith. Call me,' is fine. Give the surname unless you have an unusual first name or are very sure your friend knows who you are.

This may sound obvious, but don't ever leave a message that would be indiscreet for another person to hear. You don't know who might listen to it first and even if your friend lives alone others might be present when the machine is checked. Don't ever leave unexpected bad news on an answering machine. For example, it's all right to say, 'I've checked and I definitely can't come – sorry,' but not, 'You're fired,' or 'I've just found your cat's dead body in the gutter.'

Your own Answering Machine

Try to have a simple, clear message. It doesn't do any harm every so often to call your own number from a payphone at a major railway station – you might be surprised by the lack of clarity.

Mobile Phones

These arouse terrifically strong feelings, but from an etiquette point of view the rules are quite simple. Don't use them where they will disturb and bother others, keep your voice down when talking, and switch the phone off in any place where a modicum of quiet could be expected: theatre, cinema or concert hall; church; restaurant. There are places where using a mobile phone could be dangerous – hospitals, aircraft, petrol stations – and you must always keep to the rules. Also, it's rude to take calls on your mobile if the people you are with could expect your undivided attention – which means almost all social situations.

25

INTRODUCTIONS AND MEETING PEOPLE

There are traditional etiquette rules about introductions, and some people no doubt still stick to them, but on the whole today the important thing is to remember the names and to say them clearly at the right time – most people won't even notice if you don't get quite the correct order.

In theory you present a younger/junior/male person to an older/senior/female. Of course, even for real sticklers for correct form, it isn't always immediately obvious who was the more senior, etc. This is one of the great etiquette problems. But nowadays you need not worry too much. You say, 'Do you two know each other? This is Mary O'Donnell, my brother Joe's wife, and John Smith, whom I used to work with.' Information is more important than strict etiquette.

If you are out with a friend and you meet your boss, then you say, 'Mrs Jones [or Sally], this is my friend, Monica Thomas.' If her husband is with her and you know him, then what you say is, 'This is Mr and Mrs Jones – I work for Mrs Jones – this is my friend Monica Thomas.' If she doesn't share his name, or you don't know her companion, you say the first introduction outlined above, and it is up to her to introduce. Or you can turn to him and say, 'I'm sorry, I don't know your name,' so he can introduce himself.

Parents
How do you introduce your parents? It can feel odd saying, 'My parents, Robert and Elizabeth Browning,' but 'Mr and Mrs Browning,' could sound over-formal, and not to say a name at

all sounds odder once you're grown up (whoever you've met may not remember or know your own surname anyway and may be stuck). It's obviously particularly important to get the name in somewhere if your parents, for whatever reason, don't share your surname.

A lot of people do introduce their parents with just, 'This is my mother and father,' which is completely understandable, but then they cannot complain if the names go wrong.

I once met a friend's mother, without any formal introduction, and was terribly proud that I managed to dredge from some-where my friend's maiden name (I hadn't known her before she was married) and so I threw in lots of 'Yes, Mrs Brown' to show off. It was some time before I discovered she was actually Lady Brown. But I don't see what else any of us could have done. There was no way I could have known, and not many people nowadays would introduce themselves by their title in such a social situation, and correcting me would be hard for someone so polite. (Many years ago a journalist in a new foreign posting was issued an invitation for 'You and Mrs X to come over some time.' Deciding it was best to get this straight from the beginning, Mr X said, 'We'd love to, but I think I ought to tell you that she's not Mrs X . . .' but before he could go on to say she was Lady Patricia, his new friend interrupted to say, 'That's all right old man, we're terribly broad-minded round here, no-one'll say a word.')

In Social Groups
It's everyone's job to perform introductions. You say, 'I'm Emma, who are you?' and you say 'Barbara, do you know Matty?' every time someone new joins the group. (It's no problem if they turn out to know each other better than they know you.)

Forgotten Names
In any group larger than two, it's easy to say, 'I'm Alexander . . .' and then questioningly look at the next person, forcing him to say his own name, your look implying that you could perfectly well say it yourself but have decided it'll be more fun to play the round game. In fact, if you can see people heading for you whose names you've forgotten you can pre-empt trouble by organizing general introductions.

If you can see other people going into name-blankness rou-tines, then help out, speak your name loudly and clearly, don't rely on others to say it for you unless you're sure that's what they want to do.

A specific situation: when you take your partner to an event with people you see often but they don't (office party, evening class drinks), then do keep introducing him/her. You may feel that you've brought your partner before and you mention the name about twice an hour at work. However, your colleagues are meeting twenty colleagues' partners, can't quite remember whether it's Robin or Robert, and are anyway terrified of saying, 'I met you last year Steve, didn't I?' in case Steve has long disappeared from every area of your life except the jealous mind of your new boyfriend. Even if they're sure, there's no harm done if you say, 'You remember my fiancée, Drusilla?' They can say, 'Of course, I do,' (and nobody says that more convincingly that those who didn't remember Drusilla and are extremely grateful for your prompt).

On Being Introduced
Traditionally the two people say, 'How do you do?' and 'How do you do?' The question is, of course, a pure formality, and you should never answer it by describing your health. You can also say, 'Pleased to meet you.' This greeting is treated with suspicion in some circles and is perhaps best kept for times when there is a chance of its being true – meeting someone you've heard about or have an interest in rather than a chance acquaintance. (Though why the phrase is treated more rigorously than fake enquiries about your health I don't know.) You could also just say, 'Hello' – probably easiest, and perfectly correct.

Handshakes
Do you shake hands or kiss? Do nothing? There are no strict rules. In the old days, men shook hands with each other. A woman might shake hands with a man, but the impetus must come from her: he wouldn't stick his hand out until she'd made the first move. Women rarely shook hands with each other.

Nowadays this is all in the melting-pot. Shaking hands was seen as rather formal at one time, but there has been perhaps a swing back, on the grounds that it is nice to make some gesture of greeting and friendship, and there isn't always much of an alternative. If you don't shake hands, try at least to smile and nod at people when you're introduced. It's a great help not to be embarrassed by handshaking because it simply is a very useful gesture, particularly when you are greeting someone of a different generation or wish to show friendliness, or pleasure at meeting or re-meeting someone, but don't think that kisses are appropriate.

In business, handshaking is common and usual, and in this circumstance a man would treat a woman as a businessperson and assume he would shake hands with her. (Even socially this is often true nowadays.) You can make your own mind up whether to initiate a handshake, but the really important etiquette matter is that you get your hand out fast when someone else sticks his out. That's what really matters, that you stay reasonably alert. Sticking your hand out to someone who doesn't respond is rather mortifying. This may land you in the position that you've shaken hands with some of a group during introductions but not others, and this can feel odd, but it's nothing to worry about.

Limp handshakes are a cliché and a joke but they *are* off-putting and can seem unfriendly or stand-offish. Don't grab or squeeze, but don't let your hand simply hang there for the other person to shake. If you're worried about clammy palms, then discreetly wipe your hand on your skirt or trousers before shaking – it can be merely part of the movement of bringing your hand up.

You should really try not to shake hands with gloves on, but if it's going to hold everyone up while you undo four buttons, or you need two hands to remove and the other hand is full, then shake with gloves on.

Men used to raise (or touch) their hats on being introduced to a lady, and remove them if they were staying in her presence, so if you are the rare man who wears a hat you can practise this (most women will appreciate it). It's not truly compulsory any more though.

Kissing

This is something that bothers some people a lot and others not at all. It has undoubtedly become an accepted social gesture in this country, despite some people's horror and sneers, and there is nothing wrong with it when practised properly. However, the usual etiquette rules apply: no-one should be forced to do anything he doesn't want to, but then a polite person doesn't embarrass a kisser by avoiding a kiss.

Many women friends kiss when they see each other, and kiss

platonic male friends (more serious kissing is not in this category). It is usually a kiss on, or even merely near (the famous 'kissing the air' greeting) the cheeks, and is not very tactile. The joke that women don't want their make-up ruined is actually more or less true. There isn't really any other social gesture for such pairings: handshaking might seem too formal. Male-female social kissing should be initiated by the female in general, so if you are a man you don't need to worry whether you should be kissing your friend's wife every time you see her – it's up to her to decide. Such strictly social kisses should be given and accepted casually. Accompanying hugs should be saved for very close friends, or emotional moments (such as those requiring congratulations or sympathy).

Fig. 11. A social kiss.

Social kissing should be reserved for those you know well, not someone you've just met. The only exception might be if you're hoping to make someone feel welcome (e.g. you've just been introduced to the woman who is engaged to your brother). You should also be aware that your own personal rules may not apply in other cultures. Someone from another background may be a lot more likely (so you may seem more unfriendly than you intended if you don't kiss) or a lot less likely (you may even offend his religion if you force a kiss on him) to want to kiss you, so be careful.

If someone is set on kissing you and you're not keen, you're in trouble. You can forestall them by sticking your hand out to shake but if that doesn't work there's not much you can politely do. If you are a woman trying to avoid a man's kisses, you have to be clear in your mind whether he's trying to be social or trying to be something more. If you think it's sexual in some sense, then you can politely insist that he doesn't: if you know he's merely being social, you must try not to hurt his feelings and must not be too pointed in your fending-off. (This holds true for men too, but it is less of a problem, and fewer men are put off by kissing random members of the opposite sex.)

Any polite woman will inform a man if she has left lipstick on his cheek. It is perfectly correct to remove it for him.

26

TALKING

The old rules were that you don't talk about sex, politics or money in normal social conversation. Most people would say that sticking to those rules would make life very boring, and it's true that the rules have eased considerably. But still . . .

Nosey Questions
If you must ask nosey questions (about sex, money and politics, for example), then phrase them in such a way to give the other person a get out. Nobody has to tell you anything, but people politer than you will (wrongly, in my view) be reluctant to say, 'None of your damned business.' Try to be subtle. 'Gosh, that's lovely, it must have cost a fortune,' is a lot better than, 'How much did it cost?'

Hurtful Remarks
You can't anticipate everything that might hurt or upset someone else, but there are some remarks where it doesn't take much imagination to see the pitfalls. Try to think before you speak. Don't ever ask couples about their plans to have children, except in the most vague way. (It is, interestingly, all right to ask unattached people this, because you are asking a hypothetical question. But even this might be hurtful if he is longing to find a partner and reproduce but is having no luck, or she has just had an abortion.)

You should also never presume to have insight into other people's motives: 'I suppose your career is just too important to you.' Presumably those who make such remarks are sufficiently insensitive that they're not going to mind when one day someone tells them, 'I've had seven miscarriages, three corrective operations and most recently a full hysterectomy, and it is the biggest tragedy of my life.'

Lots of people with something dreadful or sad in their lives do not want to talk about it and so you may well not have suspected, and that is their right and privilege. They most certainly do not want to be forced to spill their sorrows to correct your wrong impression of them. Don't put them in that position.

Knowing What's Best for Others
The way women, in particular, arrange their lives is up for a lot of discussion these days: changing their names, working after childbirth, paying for childcare, breastfeeding or not. Such matters are legitimate subjects for discussion in a general way, but you shouldn't criticize or judge in specific cases for two good reasons: (1) it's just none of your business and (2) you almost certainly don't know enough of the facts to judge.

Generalizations
At a social event with people you don't know, beware of making sweeping generalizations: 'Everyone who went to public school/ comprehensive school is uneducated,' or 'Anyone who pays for private medicine is mad.' Don't say these things unless you don't care about hurting people's feelings and are prepared to defend the proposition when someone opposite you says, 'You mean me?'

Health Talk
I think health talk should be the new taboo these days, although this may be a hopeless cause. Certainly, though, over the dinner table anyone who is squeamish takes precedence over those who love to discuss health matters. They just don't make good dinner subjects. In general, you might like to be wary of other health stories, for a variety of reasons.

Firstly, they may be terribly discouraging or worrying for someone, particularly when they take the form of, 'That lump on your finger? I knew someone who had that and she lost her whole hand.' It's hard to believe people think it helpful to tell you these stories, but they do.

Secondly, unless you are a doctor, you may well be giving out remarkable disinformation. Doctors tend not to tell stories like this, notably, but lay people aggressively and arrogantly tell other people medical 'facts' which simply aren't true.

Thirdly, you shouldn't really pass on very intimate and embarrassing medical details about your friends to other people who may know them slightly. Most people don't want mere acquaintances to know about their bowel arrangements or childbirth experiences.

Honesty in Conversation

When asked for an opinion from a friend on anything at all, from a dress to a lifetime partner, there is only one simple rule. If the purchase or decision is irrevocable say, 'It's fine,' without going overboard if you really don't like it/him/her. If it is not irrevocable (and not fine), then tell the truth as tactfully as you can, trying to put something positive in there if possible. One smart lady has a useful phrase for use after the first meeting with a friend's new partner, or in answer to a request for a really honest assessment. She says, 'You know me. I never think anyone is good enough for my friends, but he seems very nice.' Because she *does* always say this, and because it contains a pretty compliment, it works perfectly to maintain her integrity without causing offence.

Swearing

Someone who dislikes swearing has the right to ask you not to, and her wishes must take precedence (rather as non-smokers tend to get their way these days). However ridiculous you may think it, you don't have the right to offend someone else with swear words. And, of course, you may politely ask someone else not to swear.

You should try not to swear at people doing their jobs, such as traffic wardens, no matter how irritating they're being. Even more important, you must never swear at people junior to you at work, or those who are being paid specifically to serve you (e.g. in restaurants). Those paid more generally to serve you (e.g. gasmen) may feel able to bite back, but juniors and waitresses on the whole can't. It is the height of bad manners to swear at such people, and is nothing more or less than bullying.

What/Pardon/Excuse me

If you want someone to repeat something you didn't hear, you say, 'What?' or 'Pardon?' Those who use 'What?' are said to consider themselves to be U, or upper class, and to look down on those who say, 'Pardon?' However, in some areas and some circles 'Pardon?' is seen as more correct. You could always say, 'Excuse me?' – a good all-purpose phrase. Said interrogatively it can mean, 'Say again,' or 'I can't believe you just said that,' and said straight it's good for interrupting, trying to pass someone physically or to pass off a sneeze or any other unexpected noise.

To Avoid Unpopularity

Generally in conversation you should not flaunt your money, position or talents: you should avoid sarcastic or derogatory remarks or personal criticism; and try not to be racist or sexist.

27

THE CLASS QUESTION

Half the time people carry on as if we lived in a classless society these days, but the rest of the time those people are having quiet, secret conversations about who others are and where they came from.

The first thing to say is that no-one should be ashamed of who they are and where they've come from: and that applies to the sons of princes as much as to slum children. Anyone who laughs at you or sneers, or makes assumptions about you based solely on your name, accent or income, is being very impolite and is someone you need not bother with. The best advice is never to pretend to be anything you aren't and never to bother what anyone else thinks. But that's obviously counsel of perfection, and most people can only aim for such objectivity. And there is always the classic case of fearing to seem to let someone else down: your new friend or fiancé loves you for yourself but you fear meeting his or her other friends or family.

Sneering at the upper classes is a real phenomenon, but unlikely to be such a problem. This is probably because money is assumed to go with such a background, and money smoothes things over for two reasons: it gives the possessor confidence (so he doesn't care if his father-in-law hates him as a poncey toff) and, most regrettably, it helps make people popular. So, in general, I will be dealing with the idea of people trying to make their way in what they (or some people) would perceive as being a higher class than they were born into.

Of course, we've all read or seen the old stories of rich families filled with consternation at the idea of a lower class friend for little Johnny, let alone a girlfriend, but this isn't nearly as prevalent these days. This is partly because history shows that anyone can be a bad friend, a bad influence: money and social cachet protect no-one. In truth, families hope most of all that its members' friends are people they can like and respect, who are polite and pleasant, and who don't take drugs or commit crimes. A friend or romantic partner like this is greeted with sighs of relief, no matter what the background. Always remember this fact.

Accents

The crazy thing in Britain is that perceived class divisions are based on a fairly arbitrary division of accents: Received Pronunciation is always seen as all right, and then regional accents are divided into OK and not-OK. Some accents are seen as ugly and lower class (Liverpool, Birmingham), whereas others (almost any Scottish accent, almost any rural accent) are seen as attractive. This plainly bears no relation to actual background or income, but is undoubtedly very widespread in Britain.

Communication is the only really important factor; if people can understand you easily that's all that matters. But if you want to change your accent, then that is entirely up to you and there is nothing wrong with that. You can have lessons in speech, or acting lessons (a good drama coach would advise and help on a voice and there isn't the same stigma or air of social climbing that 'elocution' still has). Alternatively, if you're sure what you want to achieve, you can use a tape recorder to alter your own speech – perhaps with the help of tapes from the radio of voices you like and admire.

Contrary to what people may tell you, it is not at all difficult to lose or change an accent. Anyone who has moved to a new area with a distinctive accent must have noticed how little bits of it appear in their own speech in no time at all and without trying. Think what you can do if you try. Don't believe anyone who says you are being affected or losing your roots if you change the way you speak.

If people ask about your accent or words that you use, don't get defensive and assume that they're sneering or laughing at you. These days they're almost certainly merely interested. If people pronounce a word differently from how you say it, then ask about it. Say, 'I always pronounce that scone. Do you think it's a regional difference?' or 'I'm never sure what the correct pronunciation is – controversy?' No-one will mind, and you may well find people admitting to all kinds of insecurities and uncertainties of their own. There is no shame in saying, 'I've

only ever read that word, so I don't know how it's pronounced.'
Dictionaries tell you how to pronounce words: you need to look
up the rules at the beginning of the book and then look up your
word and compare the codes and marks they use with those
listed at the front. It's complicated, but not difficult.

Going to Stay Somewhere Grand
If you are staying in a grand house as the guest of one of the
family, then you should consult your friend about everything
you want to know, same as you would if staying with a friend in
a semi in north London or a tenement in Edinburgh. He or she
will be ready and glad to help. Always remember the basics:
make your arrangements (arrival and departure times) and any
important requirements clear; bring a small gift if appropriate;
say 'please' and 'thank you'; and thank your hostess afterwards
as you leave and later with a letter. Keep alert generally and, if
you wish, copy the behaviour of someone who seems to have
good manners. Read the section on staying with older friends for
more hints.

Servants
If you have to deal with servants and you aren't sure what to do,
then the best advice is to treat them as you would a waiter or
barmaid in a restaurant. They are not your inferiors, just people
trying to do a job, so you treat them politely and say 'please' and
'thank you'. You aren't paying them directly, but they are
employed to serve you so you have an obligation to be polite but
not to be over-friendly – don't be as grateful as you would be if a
friend had brought you tea in bed or cleaned your shoes. You
ask them for anything you need, and you can even ask them for
vague advice or information ('What time is dinner? Will there be
extra guests? Is everyone changing?' are reasonable questions.
'Will old Mrs Kent be drunk again? Is that Joan woman the
Earl's mistress?' are not.)

    You do not have to leave tips for general household staff, but
if anyone was particularly helpful, or obviously was given more
work by your presence, then a fiver is a good idea. You would
expect to reward your loader on a shooting weekend. In all cases
you could consult your host for guidance. If you don't want to
hand it over directly, you could put the money in an envelope
with the recipient's name on and leave it on the bedside table or
with your host.

The Lavatory

If you want to use the lavatory, then you could ask for the bathroom, or to wash your hands (though that risks you being shown into a room with a basin and bath only). There's nothing wrong with asking for the lavatory, but the easiest and best option is probably to ask for the loo – inoffensive and universally understood. 'Toilet' just doesn't sound right.

Meals

They can be the most nerve-racking part of a visit, but try to calm down (and don't get so nervous that you drink too much . . .). Ask, if anything is unclear to you. Virtually every household has slightly different arrangements: it is not an admission of coming from a slum to ask a question. Watch what others do at all times. Some families will have more formal mealtimes than you, but it's unlikely to be anything you can't cope with (and they're not terribly likely to hate you just for getting it wrong). It's worth finding out in advance about changing for dinner – make sure you get a full answer from your friend or whoever invited you, so you're not caught out.

Some well-brought-up people put salt on the side of their plate and take it from there as they need it, as opposed to sprinkling it over their food. They may use a separate knife for bread and butter, and a teaspoon to ladle out jam. At home you may use the one knife for everything including getting out the jam. Try it their way (it's not hard) but don't panic if you forget. Other bread rules: people break rolls rather than cut them up, and put butter and jam on the side of the plate before putting it directly onto the bread. None of this is either essential or anything to worry about.

What You Call Meals

Everyone eats breakfast in the morning, but do you have lunch or dinner at midday? Tea or high tea or dinner in the evening? Neither is right or wrong, but in more upmarket circles lunch or luncheon comes at midday (which avoids confusion – nobody's in any doubt when lunch is). Tea is generally tea and cakes at 4 pm. Evening meal is dinner (if heavy or formal) or supper (if light or casual). As ever, the important thing is that there's no misunderstanding. (You're not arriving at the wrong time for a meal or expecting something more or less substantial than you get.) There is nothing to be ashamed of. Customs vary and you

Fig. 12. Good table manners: the salt is on the side of the plate; the roll has been broken, not cut; the knife on the side plate has been used only for the roll and butter; a spoon is used to take the jam out from the pot.

can say, 'Oh, we call that tea at home.' (You can say it's because you come from Yorkshire if you do.)

Last Word

I would like to stress again: so long as you talk clearly and can be understood, so long as you are polite in a natural and thoughtful way, so long as you try to be reasonably kind and pleasant to everyone (whatever their age, social class, income or working status), then you can get by anywhere in Britain or in any other country. Those are the attributes that people look for and appreciate, and they don't really care where or how you learnt them.

INDEX